100 Cross-Stitch Gifts from Nature

The Vanessa-Ann Collection

Sedgewood® Press

New York

100 Cross-Stitch Gifts from Nature

To Julie and Susan,

This dedication is our grand applause to two of the main characters in our unfolding story. Without your artistic markings on each and every book, our pages would seem bare.

Love, J and T

For Sedgewood® Press

Director: ELIZABETH P. RICE
Manager, Product Development: PATRICIA VAN NOTE
Editorial Assistant: KATHLEEN GANNON
Production Manager: BILL ROSE

For The Vanessa-Ann Collection®

Owners: TERRECE BEESLEY WOODRUFF
and JO PACKHAM

Staff: GLORIA BAUR
           BECKY BROTHERSON
           VICKI BURKE
           HOLLY FULLER
           KRISTEN JARCHOW
           SUSAN JORGENSEN
           MARGARET MARTI
           BARBARA MILBURN
           PAMELA RANDALL
           JULIE TRUMAN
           NANCY WHITLEY

Designers: TRICE BOERENS
            DALE BRYNER
            MARY CALE
            VICKIE EVERHART
            TINA RICHARDS
            JULIE TRUMAN
            TERRECE WOODRUFF

Photographer: RYNE HAZEN

Much of the photography for this book was done at Mary Gaskill's **Trends and Traditions**, part of Historic 25th Street; Ogden, Utah. Other photographs were taken at Ivywood in Ogden, Utah, and at the homes of Jo Lynn Bushnell, Edie Stockstill, Susan Whitelock, and Mary Ann Wright.

The Vanessa-Ann Collection expresses its thanks for their cooperation.

First Printing 1989
Library of Congress Catalog number: 88-062567
ISBN: 0-696-02328-8
Published by Sedgewood® Press

Distributed by Meredith Corporation, Des Moines, Iowa.

10 9 8 7 6 5 4 3 2 1

In the shadows of Utah's majestic Wasatch Rocky Mountains, the four seasons are painted in a distinct and brilliant variety of ever-changing colors and textures. Being surrounded by Nature, we have chosen to portray her wonders through the eyes of a cross-stitcher.

Nature bestows her gifts to us throughout the year, time after time. Trees stretch to the sky, birds greet the dawn, flowers flaunt their colors and tempt us to partake in the unfolding drama. Though, as one season moves to the next, we sometimes long to save and share these memorable moments.

In reflecting upon the past year, we lovingly gathered our memories. Then, as our gift to you, we have recreated some of nature's finest offerings and displayed them in vivid colors and a variety of textures. Now you, in turn, can stitch these treasures to give to special friends and family throughout every season of the year!

CONTENTS

SPRING ❧ SUMMER

A U T U M N ❧ W I N T E R

SPRING

FROM ABC TO Z

FABRIC	DESIGN SIZES
Aida 11	3⅝" × 3⅝"
Aida 14	2⅞" × 2⅞"
Aida 18	2¼" × 2¼"
Hardanger 22	1⅞" × 1⅞"

ANCHOR   DMC (used for sample)

Step One: Cross-stitch (two strands)

893	+	224	Shell Pink-lt.
894	△	223	Shell Pink-med.
869	○	3042	Antique Violet-lt.
871	∴	3041	Antique Violet-med.
900	—	928	Slate Green-lt.
875	■	503	Blue Green-med.
842	✕	3013	Khaki Green-lt.
859	●	3052	Gray Green-med.

Step Two: Backstitch (one strand)

| 878 | 501 | Blue Green-dk. |

ANCHOR   DMC (used for sample)

Step One: Cross-stitch (two strands)

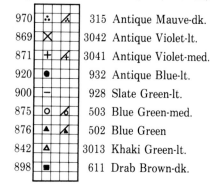

970	∴ ╱	315	Antique Mauve-dk.
869	✕	3042	Antique Violet-lt.
871	+ ╱	3041	Antique Violet-med.
920	●	932	Antique Blue-lt.
900	—	928	Slate Green-lt.
875	○ ╱	503	Blue Green-med.
876	▲ ╱	502	Blue Green
842	△	3013	Khaki Green-lt.
898	■	611	Drab Brown-dk.

Step Two: Backstitch (one strand)

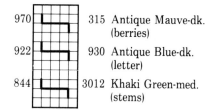

970	315	Antique Mauve-dk. (berries)
922	930	Antique Blue-dk. (letter)
844	3012	Khaki Green-med. (stems)

Stitch Count: 40 × 40

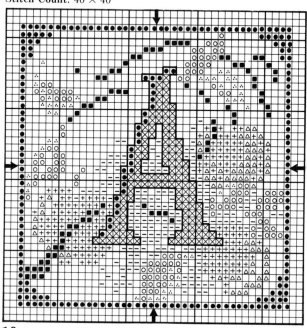

Stitch Count: 40 × 40

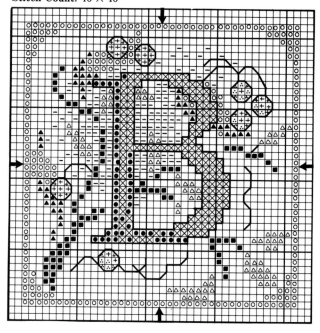

ANCHOR   DMC (used for sample)

Step One: Cross-stitch (two strands)

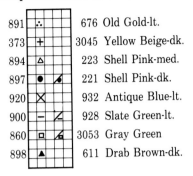

891	∴		676	Old Gold-lt.
373	+		3045	Yellow Beige-dk.
894	△		223	Shell Pink-med.
897	●	╱	221	Shell Pink-dk.
920	✕		932	Antique Blue-lt.
900	–	╱	928	Slate Green-lt.
860	▫	╱	3053	Gray Green
898	▲		611	Drab Brown-dk.

Step Two: Backstitch (one strand)

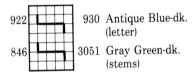

| 922 | | 930 | Antique Blue-dk. (letter) |
| 846 | | 3051 | Gray Green-dk. (stems) |

ANCHOR   DMC (used for sample)

Step One: Cross-stitch (two strands)

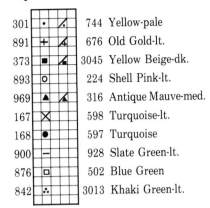

301	•	╱	744	Yellow-pale
891	+	◢	676	Old Gold-lt.
373	■	◣	3045	Yellow Beige-dk.
893	○		224	Shell Pink-lt.
969	▲	◣	316	Antique Mauve-med.
167	✕		598	Turquoise-lt.
168	●		597	Turquoise
900	–		928	Slate Green-lt.
876	▫		502	Blue Green
842	∴		3013	Khaki Green-lt.

Step Two: Backstitch (one strand)

| 373 | | 3045 | Yellow Beige-dk. (daisy) |
| 168 | | 597 | Turquoise (letter) |

Stitch Count: 40 × 40

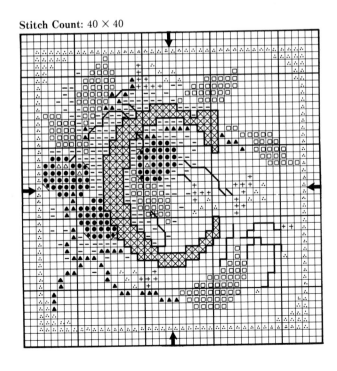

Stitch Count: 40 × 40

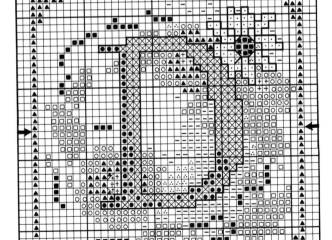

11

ANCHOR   DMC (used for sample)

Step One: Cross-stitch (two strands)

1	· ╱		White
891	✕	676	Old Gold-lt.
373	▵ ╱	3045	Yellow Beige-dk.
893	∴	224	Shell Pink-lt.
869	▫	3042	Antique Violet-lt.
871	▲	3041	Antique Violet-med.
920	○	932	Antique Blue-lt.
900	—	928	Slate Green-lt.
875	+	503	Blue Green-med.
379	■ ╱	840	Beige Brown-med.

Step Two: Backstitch (one strand)

373		3045	Yellow Beige-dk. (letter)
876		502	Blue Green (stems)
379		840	Beige Brown-med. (eggs and nest)

ANCHOR   DMC (used for sample)

Step One: Cross-stitch (two strands)

969	✕	316	Antique Mauve-med.
970	●	315	Antique Mauve-dk.
871	+	3041	Antique Violet-med.
900	—	928	Slate Green-lt.
842	○	3013	Khaki Green-lt.
860	▫	3053	Gray Green
378	■	841	Beige Brown-lt.

Step Two: Backstitch (one strand)

970		315	Antique Mauve-dk.

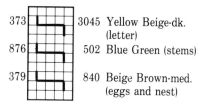

Stitch Count: 40 × 40

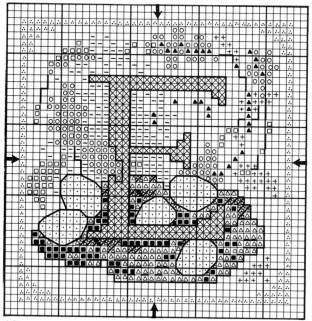

Stitch Count: 40 × 40

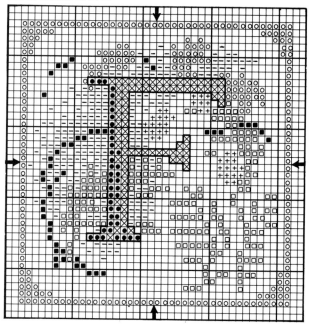

ANCHOR DMC (used for sample)

Step One: Cross-stitch (two strands)

ANCHOR			DMC	
871	∴	◿	3041	Antique Violet-med.
920	✕		932	Antique Blue-lt.
921	●		931	Antique Blue-med.
900	−	◿	928	Slate Green-lt.
844	+	◿	3012	Khaki Green-med.
846	○	◿	3051	Gray Green-dk.
379	■		840	Beige Brown-med.

Step Two: Backstitch (one strand)

862	⌐	520	Fern Green-dk.

ANCHOR DMC (used for sample)

Step One: Cross-stitch (two strands)

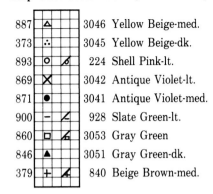

ANCHOR			DMC	
887	△		3046	Yellow Beige-med.
373	∴		3045	Yellow Beige-dk.
893	○	◿	224	Shell Pink-lt.
869	✕		3042	Antique Violet-lt.
871	●		3041	Antique Violet-med.
900	−	◿	928	Slate Green-lt.
860	□	◿	3053	Gray Green
846	▲		3051	Gray Green-dk.
379	+	◿	840	Beige Brown-med.

Step Two: Backstitch (one strand)

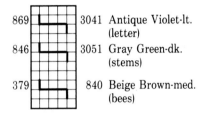

869	⌐	3041	Antique Violet-lt. (letter)
846	⌐	3051	Gray Green-dk. (stems)
379	⌐	840	Beige Brown-med. (bees)

Stitch Count: 40 × 40

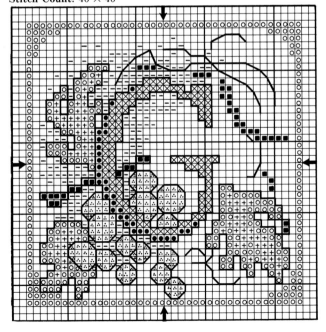

Stitch Count: 40 × 40

13

ANCHOR DMC (used for sample)

Step One: Cross-stitch (two strands)

301	☒	744	Yellow-pale
891	●	676	Old Gold-lt.
869	+	3042	Antique Violet-lt.
871	∴	3041	Antique Violet-med.
167	○	598	Turquoise-lt.
900	–	928	Slate Green-lt.
876	■	502	Blue Green
842	▢	3013	Khaki Green-lt.
860	▲	3053	Gray Green

Step Two: Backstitch (one strand)

878		501	Blue Green-dk. (iris, stems)
860		3053	Gray Green (letter)

ANCHOR DMC (used for sample)

Step One: Cross-stitch (two strands)

891	○	676	Old Gold-lt.
893	∴	224	Shell Pink-lt.
894	+	223	Shell Pink-med.
869	▲	3042	Antique Violet-lt.
900	–	928	Slate Green-lt.
213	☒	504	Blue Green-lt.
876	■	502	Blue Green
842	▢	3013	Khaki Green-lt.

Step Two: Backstitch (one strand)

922		930	Antique Blue-dk.

Stitch Count: 40 × 40

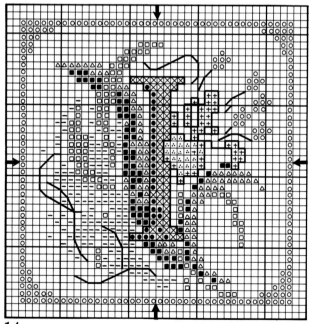

Stitch Count: 40 × 40

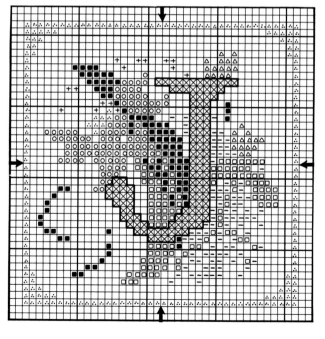

ANCHOR   DMC (used for sample)

Step One: Cross-stitch (two strands)

887	+	3046	Yellow Beige-med.
893	✕	224	Shell Pink-lt.
969	△	316	Antique Mauve-med.
970	●	315	Antique Mauve-dk.
920	○	932	Antique Blue-lt.
900	–	928	Slate Green-lt.
842	∴	3013	Khaki Green-lt.
860	·	3053	Gray Green
846	▫	3051	Gray Green-dk.

Step Two: Backstitch (one strand)

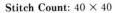

970	⌐	315	Antique Mauve-dk. (letter)
846	⌐	3051	Gray Green-dk. (stems)

ANCHOR   DMC (used for sample)

Step One: Cross-stitch (two strands)

1	·	╱		White
886	○		677	Old Gold-vy. lt.
869	∴	╱	3042	Antique Violet-lt.
167	▲		598	Turquoise-lt.
920	✕		932	Antique Blue-lt.
921	●		931	Antique Blue-lt.
900	–		928	Slate Green-lt.
875	+		503	Blue Green-med.
876	▫		502	Blue Green

Step Two: Backstitch (one strand)

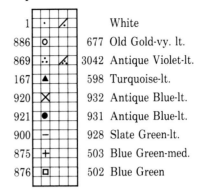

921	⌐	931	Antique Blue-med.

Stitch Count: 40 × 40

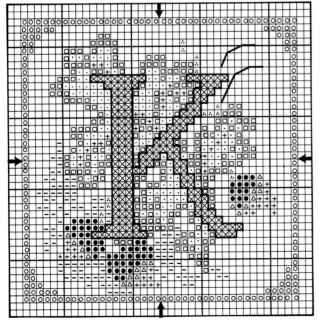

Stitch Count: 40 × 40

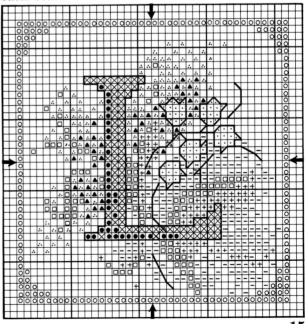

15

ANCHOR   DMC (used for sample)

Step One: Cross-stitch (two strands)

Anchor	Symbol	DMC	Color
887	⊙ ／	3046	Yellow Beige-med.
869	＋	3042	Antique Violet-lt.
5975	△	356	Terra Cotta-med.
882	∴	407	Sportsman Flesh-dk.
900	－	928	Slate Green-lt.
842	✕	3013	Khaki Green-lt.
844	●	3012	Khaki Green-med.
379	■	840	Beige Brown-med.

Step Two: Backstitch (one strand)

Anchor	DMC	Color
845	3011	Khaki Green-dk. (letter)
846	3051	Gray Green-dk. (stems)

ANCHOR   DMC (used for sample)

Step One: Cross-stitch (two strands)

Anchor	Symbol	DMC	Color
887	·	3046	Yellow Beige-med.
893	＋	224	Shell Pink-lt.
869	✕	3042	Antique Violet-lt.
871	●	3041	Antique Violet-med.
920	∴ ／	932	Antique Blue-lt.
167	○	598	Turquoise-lt.
900	－	928	Slate Green-lt.
844	□	3012	Khaki Green-med.
379	■	840	Beige Brown-med.

Step Two: Backstitch (one strand)

Anchor	DMC	Color
373	3045	Yellow Beige-dk. (nest)
871	3041	Antique Violet-med. (letter)

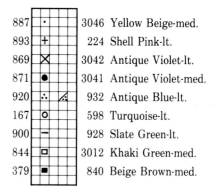

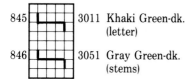

Stitch Count: 40 × 40

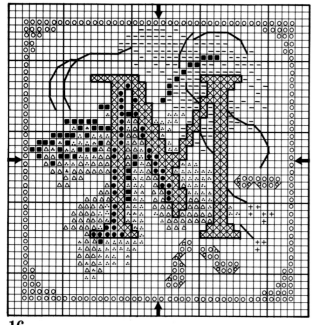

Stitch Count: 40 × 40

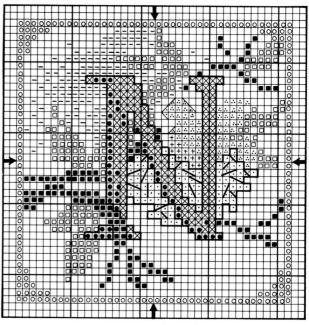

ANCHOR DMC (used for sample)

Step One: Cross-stitch (two strands)

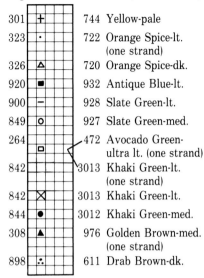

301	+	744 Yellow-pale
323	·	722 Orange Spice-lt. (one strand)
326	△	720 Orange Spice-dk.
920	■	932 Antique Blue-lt.
900	−	928 Slate Green-lt.
849	○	927 Slate Green-med.
264	□	472 Avocado Green-ultra lt. (one strand)
842		3013 Khaki Green-lt. (one strand)
842	✕	3013 Khaki Green-lt.
844	●	3012 Khaki Green-med.
308	▲	976 Golden Brown-med. (one strand)
898	∴	611 Drab Brown-dk.

Step Two: Backstitch (one strand)

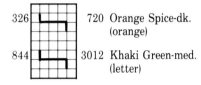

| 326 | 720 Orange Spice-dk. (orange) |
| 844 | 3012 Khaki Green-med. (letter) |

ANCHOR DMC (used for sample)

Step One: Cross-stitch (two strands)

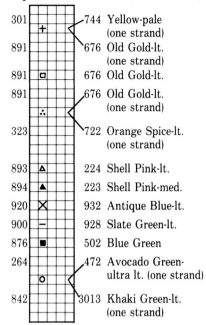

301	+	744 Yellow-pale (one strand)
891		676 Old Gold-lt. (one strand)
891	□	676 Old Gold-lt.
891	∴	676 Old Gold-lt. (one strand)
323		722 Orange Spice-lt. (one strand)
893	△	224 Shell Pink-lt.
894	▲	223 Shell Pink-med.
920	✕	932 Antique Blue-lt.
900	−	928 Slate Green-lt.
876	■	502 Blue Green
264	○	472 Avocado Green-ultra lt. (one strand)
842		3013 Khaki Green-lt. (one strand)

Step Two: Backstitch (one strand)

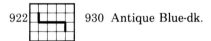

| 922 | 930 Antique Blue-dk. |

Stitch Count: 40 × 40

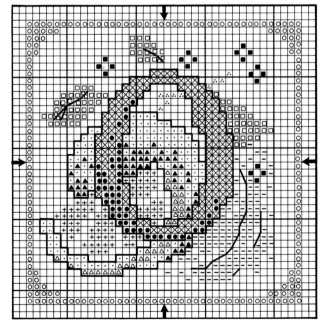

Stitch Count: 40 × 40

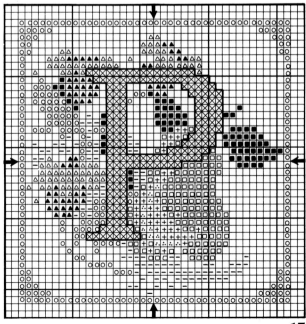

ANCHOR DMC (used for sample)

Step One: Cross-stitch (two strands)

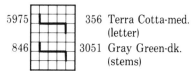

Anchor	Symbol	DMC	Color
891	○	676	Old Gold-lt.
5975	●	356	Terra Cotta-med.
882	✕	407	Sportsman Flesh-dk.
900	−	928	Slate Green-lt.
842	△	3013	Khaki Green-lt.
860	■	3053	Gray Green
378	∴	841	Beige Brown-lt.

Step Two: Backstitch (one strand)

Anchor		DMC	Color
5975		356	Terra Cotta-med. (letter)
846		3051	Gray Green-dk. (stems)

ANCHOR DMC (used for sample)

Step One: Cross-stitch (two strands)

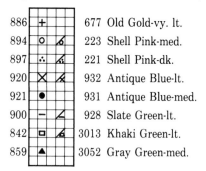

Anchor	Symbol	DMC	Color
886	+	677	Old Gold-vy. lt.
894	○ ⁄	223	Shell Pink-med.
897	∴ ⁄	221	Shell Pink-dk.
920	✕ ⁄	932	Antique Blue-lt.
921	●	931	Antique Blue-med.
900	− ⁄	928	Slate Green-lt.
842	□ ⁄	3013	Khaki Green-lt.
859	▲	3052	Gray Green-med.

Step Two: Backstitch (one strand)

Anchor		DMC	Color
921		931	Antique Blue-med. (letter)
862		520	Fern Green-dk. (stems)

Stitch Count: 40 × 40

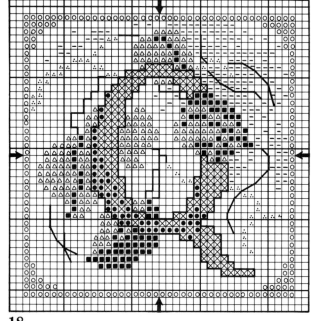

Stitch Count: 40 × 40

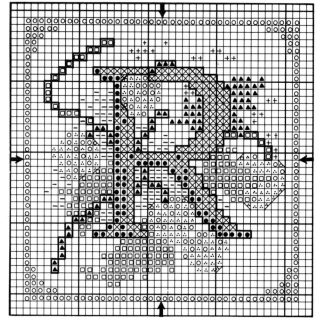

ANCHOR   DMC (used for sample)

Step One: Cross-stitch (two strands)

887	○	3046 Yellow Beige-med.
894	+	223 Shell Pink-med.
897	□	221 Shell Pink-dk.
920	✕	932 Antique Blue-lt.
921	●	931 Antique Blue-med.
900	−	928 Slate Green-lt.
859	△	3052 Gray Green-med.
846	∴	3051 Gray Green-dk.
898	■	611 Drab Brown-dk.

Step Two: Backstitch (one strand)

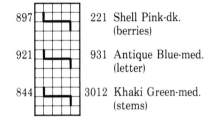

897	221 Shell Pink-dk. (berries)
921	931 Antique Blue-med. (letter)
844	3012 Khaki Green-med. (stems)

Step Three: French Knots (one strand)

897	●	221 Shell Pink-dk.

ANCHOR   DMC (used for sample)

Step One: Cross-stitch (two strands)

893	+	224 Shell Pink-lt.
894	✕	223 Shell Pink-med.
897	●	221 Shell Pink-dk.
969	□	316 Antique Mauve-med.
970	▲	315 Antique Mauve-dk.
920	○	932 Antique Blue-lt.
900	−	928 Slate Green-lt.
842	∴	3013 Khaki Green-lt.
859	△	3052 Gray Green-med.
846	■	3051 Gray Green-dk.

Step Two: Backstitch (one strand)

897	221 Shell Pink-dk. (letter)
846	3051 Gray Green-dk. (stems)

Stitch Count: 40 × 40

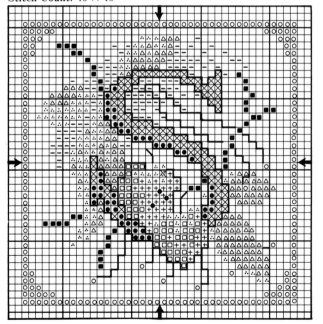

Stitch Count: 40 × 40

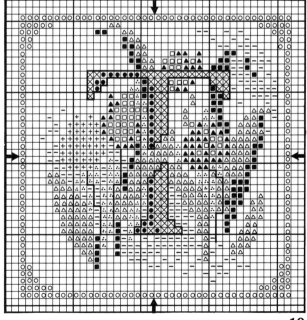

ANCHOR/DMC (used for sample)

Step One: Cross-stitch (two strands)

1	·	White
301	●	744 Yellow-pale
891	✕	676 Old Gold-lt.
869	○	3042 Antique Violet-lt.
158	+	775 Baby Blue-lt.
900	−	928 Slate Green-lt.
842	▫	3013 Khaki Green-lt.
859	∴	3052 Gray Green-med.
846	▲	3051 Gray Green-dk.
379	■	840 Beige Brown-med.

Step Two: Backstitch (one strand)

846		3051 Gray Green-dk.

ANCHOR/DMC (used for sample)

Step One: Cross-stitch (two strands)

891	○	676 Old Gold-lt.
869	✕	3042 Antique Violet-lt.
871	▲	3041 Antique Violet-med.
900	−	928 Slate Green-lt.
860	+	3053 Gray Green
859	△	3052 Gray Green-med.
846	■	3051 Gray Green-dk.

Step Two: Backstitch (one strand)

871		3041 Antique Violet-med. (letter)
846		3051 Gray Green-dk. (stems)

Stitch Count: 40 × 40

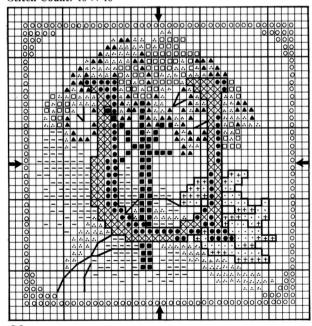

Stitch Count: 40 × 40

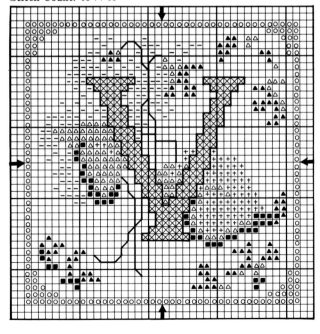

ANCHOR   DMC (used for sample)

Step One: Cross-stitch (two strands)

1	·	White
892	+	225 Shell Pink-vy. lt.
893	o	224 Shell Pink-lt.
869	▲	3042 Antique Violet-lt.
167	□	598 Turquoise-lt.
168	∴	597 Turquoise
900	−	928 Slate Green-lt.
875	✕	503 Blue Green-med.
876	●	502 Blue Green

Step Two: Backstitch (one strand)

893		224 Shell Pink-lt. (flowers)
878		501 Blue Green-dk. (letter)

ANCHOR   DMC (used for sample)

Step One: Cross-stitch (two strands)

886	+		677 Old Gold-vy. lt.
893	□	◿	224 Shell Pink-lt.
894	▲	◤	223 Shell Pink-med.
969	o		316 Antique Mauve-med.
869	∴		3042 Antique Violet-lt.
842	△		3013 Khaki Green-lt.
860	■		3053 Gray Green
378	✕		841 Beige Brown-lt.
379	●		840 Beige Brown-med.

Step Two: Backstitch (one strand)

846		3051 Gray Green-dk. (stems)
379		840 Beige Brown-med. (letter)

Stitch Count: 40 × 40

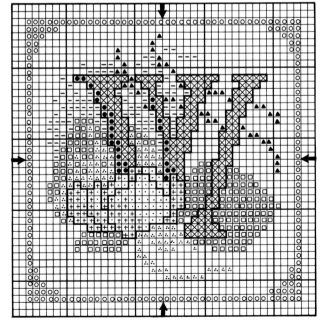

Stitch Count: 40 × 40

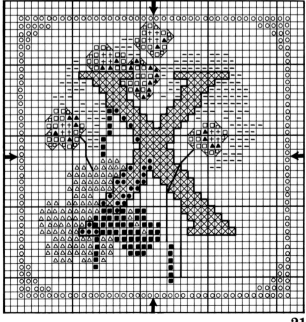

ANCHOR   DMC (used for sample)

Step One: Cross-stitch (two strands)

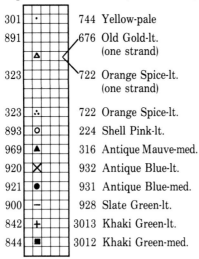

301	744	Yellow-pale
891	676	Old Gold-lt. (one strand)
323	722	Orange Spice-lt. (one strand)
323	722	Orange Spice-lt.
893	224	Shell Pink-lt.
969	316	Antique Mauve-med.
920	932	Antique Blue-lt.
921	931	Antique Blue-med.
900	928	Slate Green-lt.
842	3013	Khaki Green-lt.
844	3012	Khaki Green-med.

Step Two: Backstitch (one strand)

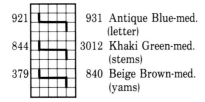

921	931	Antique Blue-med. (letter)
844	3012	Khaki Green-med. (stems)
379	840	Beige Brown-med. (yams)

ANCHOR   DMC (used for sample)

Step One: Cross-stitch (two strands)

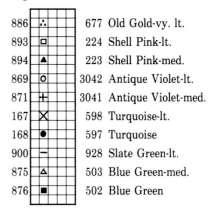

886	677	Old Gold-vy. lt.
893	224	Shell Pink-lt.
894	223	Shell Pink-med.
869	3042	Antique Violet-lt.
871	3041	Antique Violet-med.
167	598	Turquoise-lt.
168	597	Turquoise
900	928	Slate Green-lt.
875	503	Blue Green-med.
876	502	Blue Green

Step Two: Backstitch (one strand)

922	930	Antique Blue-dk. (letter)
878	501	Blue Green-dk. (stems)

Stitch Count: 40 × 40

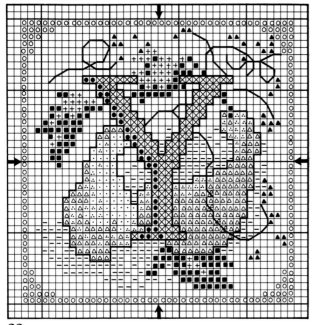

Stitch Count: 40 × 40

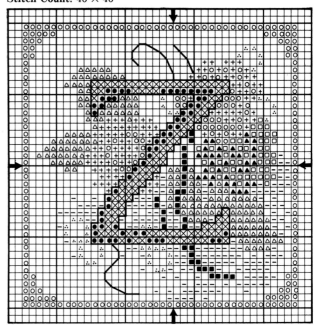

The letters P, B and J were stitched on cream Belfast Linen 32 over two threads. The finished design size for all three letters is 8⅛″ × 2½″. The fabric was cut 15″ × 9″.

The letter "G" was stitched on cream Belfast Linen 32 over two threads. The finished design size is 2½″ × 2½″. The fabric was cut 6″ × 6″.

MATERIALS for "G" pillow
Completed cross-stitch on cream Belfast Linen 32
⅜ yard of taupe fabric for pillow; matching thread
2½ yards of 1″-wide flat cream lace
½ yard of ⅜″-wide flat white lace
½ yard of ¼″-wide green with gold ribbon
2 yards of ⅛″-wide gray silk ribbon
2 yards of ⅛″-wide cream silk ribbon
2 yards of ⅛″-wide taupe silk ribbon
Thirty clear glass beads
One 10″ × 10″ knife-edge pillow form

All seam allowances are ¼″.

1 Cut linen 4″ × 4″ with design centered. Zig-zag edges. Cut two 9½″ × 9½″ pieces from taupe fabric for pillow.

2 Center design piece on one 12″ × 12″ square; baste. Place green/gold ribbon at edge of design. Stitch to pillow top. Place ⅜″-wide cream trim over seam of design piece and ribbon. Slipstitch both edges to pillow top, mitering corners. To prepare taupe ribbon, tie loose knots about 6″ apart. Then, drape in loops and folds close to inside edge of flat trim. Set aside eight glass beads. Tack ribbon to pillow top, sewing beads onto ribbon through all layers.

3 Stitch gathering threads in edge of 1″-wide cream lace. Mark four 22″ intervals. Gather lace to 36″. Placing marks at each corner, stitch lace to pillow top and disperse fullness evenly.

4 Stitch pillow back to pillow top, leaving 7″ opening. Clip corners. Turn. Insert pillow form. Slipstitch opening closed. Remove gathering threads.

5 Cut gray and cream ribbon into two 18″ pieces. Handling one gray piece and one cream piece as a set, tie ribbons into 2″-wide bow. Tack bow to center bottom edge of design. Sew four beads onto ribbon through pillow top to secure. Tie knots near ends of ribbon. Repeat process to make and secure bow for upper left corner of pillow.

The letter "S" was stitched on cream Belfast Linen 32 over two threads. The finished design size is 2½″ × 2½″. The fabric was cut 6″ × 6″.

MATERIALS for "S" square
6″ of 55″-wide cream Belfast Linen 32 (includes design and finishing); matching thread
¾ yard of 2¼″-wide gold scalloped trim
1 yard of ¼″-wide flat gold w/burgundy trim
Four purchased 2″ burgundy tassels
3 cups of sawdust
Dressmakers' pen

All seam allowances are ¼″.

1 Cut the design piece 6″ × 6″ with design centered.

2 Stitch the gusset strip to the right sides of the design piece. Stitch the back to the gusset, aligning the corners with design piece leaving a small opening. Turn.

3 Slipstitch the 2¼″-wide trim to the right side of the design piece on stitching line, beginning at a corner and folding ½″-deep inverted pleats in each corner. Stitch the flat gold trim over the top edge of the wide gold trim. Also stitch the flat trim in a square between the design and the wide gold trim.

4 Fill with sawdust. Slipstitch opening closed. Tack tassels to corners of design piece over ends of trim.

HANGING VIOLETS

Stitched on carnation pink Damask Aida 18 over one thread, the finished design size is 2⅞″ × 3½″. The fabric was cut 13″ × 13″.

FABRIC	DESIGN SIZES
Aida 11	4¾″ × 5¾″
Aida 14	3¾″ × 4⅝″
Aida 18	2⅞″ × 3½″
Hardanger 22	2⅜″ × 2⅞″

ANCHOR   DMC (used for sample)

Step One: Cross-stitch (two strands)

292	+	3078	Golden Yellow-vy. lt.
968	·	778	Antique Mauve-lt.
968	□	778	Antique Mauve-lt. (one strand)
969		316	Antique Mauve-med. (one strand)
969	✕	316	Antique Mauve-med.
970	▲	315	Antique Mauve-dk.
859	o	3052	Gray Green-med.
846	∴	3051	Gray Green-dk.
862	■	934	Black Avocado Green

Step Two: Backstitch (one strand)

| 862 | | 934 | Black Avocado Green |

MATERIALS

Completed cross-stitch on carnation pink Damask Aida 18; matching thread
¼ yard of pink fabric for lining
1¼ yards of pastel ½″-wide braid (available with upholstery supplies)
Two matching tassels
One ⅜″-wide button
1½″ piece of small elastic
Glue
Dressmakers' pen

All seam allowances are ¼″.

1 Enlarge and make pattern. Place pattern on design piece with point 4″ from top edge of design and cut one. Also cut one from lining fabric.

2 Fold with right sides together. Stitch the center back edges together. Refold with center back seam matching vertical center of design. Stitch across bottom edge. Repeat with lining.

3 Fold loop in elastic. Pin on point with loop toward design.

4 Turn design piece right side out. Slide lining over design piece, matching center back seam and top edge. Stitch top edges together, securing elastic and leaving a small opening. Clip inside corners; trim excess fabric (but not elastic) from point. Turn. Fold lining inside pocket. Slipstitch the opening closed.

5 Leaving a 6″ tail, slipstitch cord to edge of pocket, beginning at lower left corner. Allow an 11″ loop for handle and continue around to lower left corner. Knot. Also knot ends. Glue tassels to knots. Sew button to center back seam.

1 square = 1″

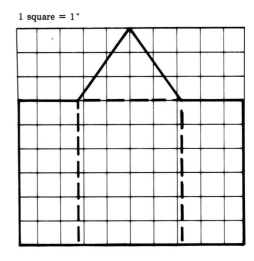

Stitch Count: 52 × 64

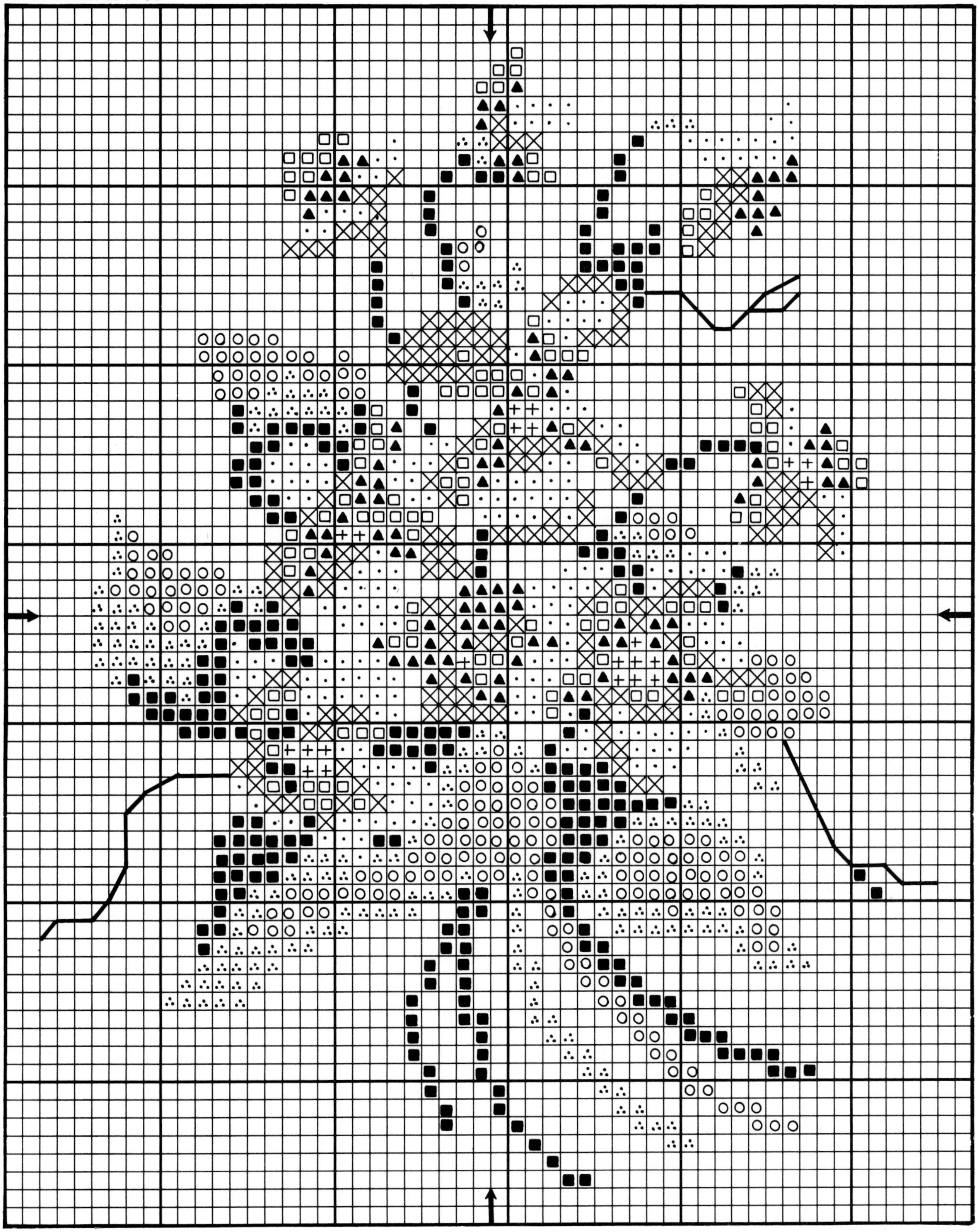

CROCHETED DUET

Stitched on ivory Lugana 25 over two threads, the finished design size for #1 is 3⅜″ × 3¼″; #2 is 2½″ × 2½″. The fabric was cut 9″ × 9″ for both.

FABRIC	DESIGN SIZES #1	DESIGN SIZES #2
Aida 11	3⅞″ × 3¾″	2⅞″ × 3″
Aida 14	3″ × 2⅞″	2¼″ × 2¼″
Aida 18	2⅜″ × 2¼″	1¾″ × 1¾″
Hardanger 22	1⅞″ × 1⅞″	1⅜″ × 1½″

ANCHOR   DMC (used for sample)

Step One: Cross-stitch (two strands)

778	−	948	Peach Flesh-vy. lt.
4146	●	950	Sportsman Flesh-lt.
900	△	928	Slate Green-lt.
849	✕	927	Slate Green-med.
875	∴	503	Blue Green-med.
859	■	3053	Gray Green

#1 Stitch Count: 42 × 41

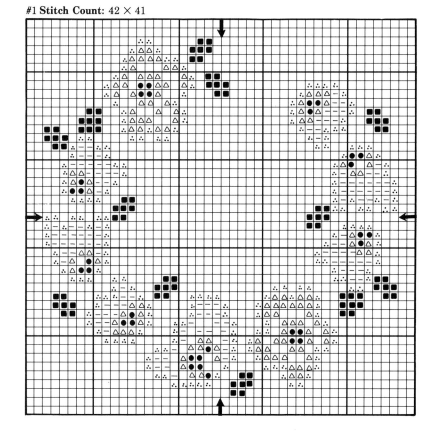

MATERIALS for doily #1
Completed cross-stitch on ivory Lugana 25
One ball of Coats & Clark #30 Ecru, 150 yards
Size 8 steel crochet hook

1 Mark a 6¾″-wide circle on fabric with design centered. Machine hemstitch at least 140 holes on line. Cut ⅜″ outside the hemstitching and zigzag raw edge.

2 Crochet the edging.

Rnd 1: Fold ⅛″ edge under and work sc in each hemstitch hole. If the number of sts is more than 140, decrease by skipping 2 sts occasionally on next rnd to get 140 sts.

Rnd 2: Ch 3, 2 dc in same st, [ch 3, sk 1 st, 3 dc in next st] around, end with ch 3, sl st in top of beg ch (70 dc groups), turn, sl st in next sp to center the st, turn again.

Rnd 3: Ch 3, 2 dc in same sp, * [ch 4, 3 dc in next sp] 4 times, [ch 5, dc in next sp] twice, ch 5, 3 dc in next sp; repeat from * around, end with (ch 5, dc in next sp) twice, ch 5, sl st in top of beg ch, sl st in next 3 sts and into next sp.

Rnd 4: Ch 3, 2 dc in same sp, * [ch 5, 3 dc in next sp] 3 times, [ch 5, sc in next sp] 3 times, ch 5, 3 dc in next sp; repeat from * around, end with [ch 5, sc in next sp] 3 times, ch 5, sl st in top of beg ch, sl st in next 3 sts and into next sp.

Rnd 5: Ch 3, 2 dc in same sp, * [ch 5, 3 dc in next sp] twice, [ch 5, sc in next sp] 4 times, ch 5, 3 dc in next sp; repeat from * around, end with [ch 5, sc in next sp] 4 times, ch 5, sl st in top of beg ch, sl st in next 3 sts and into next sp.
Continued

Rnd 6: Ch 3, 2 dc in same sp, ch 5, 3 dc in next sp, * ch 6, sc in next sp, [ch 5, sc in next sp] 4 times, ch 6, 3 dc in next sp, ch 5, 3 dc in next sp; repeat from * around, end with [ch 5, sc in next sp] 4 times, ch 6, sl st in top of beg ch, sl st in next 3 sts and into next sp.

Rnd 7: Ch 3, [3 dc, ch 6, dc in top of dc just made, 4 dc] in same sp, * ch 3, sk 1 dc, sc in next dc, ch 5, sc in next sp, ch 5, sc in same sp, [ch 5, sc in next sp] twice, ch 5, sc in same sp, sc in next sp, ch 5, sc in same sp, ch 5, sc in next sp, ch 5, sc in next sp, ch 5, sc in same sp, ch 5, sk 1 dc, sc in next dc, ch 3, [4 dc, ch 6, dc in top of dc just made, 4 dc] in next sp; repeat from * around except omit between last set of [ ] of last repeat, end with ch 3, sl st in top of beg ch.

#2 Stitch Count: 31 × 32

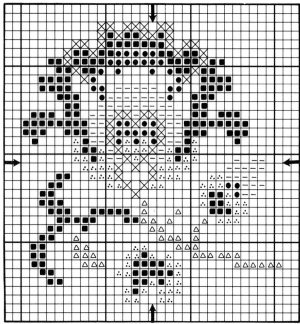

MATERIALS for doily #2
Completed cross-stitch on ivory Lugana 25
One ball of Coats & Clark #30 Ecru, 150 yards
Size 8 steel **crochet hook**

1 Mark a 6"-wide circle on fabric with design centered. Machine hemstitch at least 120 holes on line. Cut ⅜" outside the hemstitching and zigzag raw edge.

2 Crochet the edging.

Rnd 1: Fold ⅛" edge under and work sc in each hemstitch hole. If the number of sts is more than 120, decrease by skipping 2 sts occasionally on next rnd to get 120 sts.

Rnd 2: Ch 3, 2 dc in same st, dc in next st, [3 dc in next st, dc in next st] around, end with sl st in top of beg ch.

Rnd 3: Ch 1, sc in the dc just completed, sc in next 4 sts, * ch 7, sk 7 sts, [dc, ch 5, dc] in next st, ch 7, sk 7 sts, sc in next 5 sts; repeat from * around, except omit sc in last 5 sts of last repeat, sl st in beg sc (12 pattern sections), sl st in next sc.

Rnd 4: Ch 1, sc in same st, sc in next 2 sts, * ch 8, sk next sp, 11 dc in next sp, ch 8, sk next sp and 1 sc, sc in next 3 sts; repeat from * except omit last 3 sc of last repeat, end with sl st in beg sc, sl st in next 2 sc and next 6 ch.

Rnd 5: Ch 1, 2 sc in same ch-sp, * hdc in next 11 sts, 2 sc in next sp, ch 12, 2 sc in next sp; repeat from * around, except end with ch 12, sl st in beg ch 1, sl st in next 2 sts.

Rnd 6: Ch 4, sk 1 st, dc in next st, [ch 1, sk 1, dc in next st] 4 times, * ch 8, [dc, ch 5, dc] in center ch of next sp, ch 8, sk 2 sc, dc in next st, [ch 1, sk 1 st, dc in next st] 5 times; repeat from * around, end with ch 8, [dc, ch 5, dc] in center of next sp, ch 8, sl st in 3rd ch of beg, sl st in next sp.

Rnd 7: Ch 2, * [2 hdc in next ch-1 sp] 3 times, hdc in next ch-1 sp, ch 7, sk next sp, [dc, ch 2, dc, ch 2, dc, ch 2, dc, ch 2, dc] in next ch-5 sp, ch 7, sk next sp, hdc in next ch-1 sp; repeat from * around, except omit last hdc of last repeat, sl st in beg ch, sl st in next st.

Rnd 8: Ch 3, holding back last loop of each dc: make a cluster as follows: [sk 1 st, dc in next st] 3 times, dc in next st. Thread over hook and pull through all 5 loops held back, * ch 4, sl st in 3rd ch from hook to form a picot, [ch 3, sl st in same ch as previous picot] 2 times, ch 7, # [2 dc, ch-3 picot, dc] in next ch-2 sp; repeat from #, 3 times, ch 7, make a cluster over next hdc section as before, holding back last loop of each dc: dc in first hdc, sk 1 st, dc in next hdc, sk 1 st, dc in next hdc, sk 1 st, dc in next two hdc, thread over hook and pull through all 6 loops on hook; repeat from * around, end with ch 7, sl st in top of beg ch. Fasten off.

JUST ENOUGH TULIPS

The tulips in the green frame (see photo) were stitched on white Dublin Linen 25 over one thread. The finished design size is 8⅜″ × 8¾″. The fabric was cut 15″ × 15″.

ANCHOR   DMC (used for sample)

Step One: Cross-stitch (one strand)

300	I	745	Yellow-lt. pale
293	▫	727	Topaz-vy. lt.
48	·	818	Baby Pink
24	O	776	Pink-med.
75	✕	604	Cranberry-lt.
76	◇	603	Cranberry
85	–	3609	Plum-ultra lt.
86	⊙	3608	Plum-vy. lt.
87	∴	3607	Plum-lt.
88	▲	718	Plum
108	+	211	Lavender-lt.
104	▽	210	Lavender-med.
105	●	209	Lavender-dk.
110	▨	208	Lavender-vy. dk.
213	⊠	369	Pistachio Green-vy. lt.
214	▪	368	Pistachio Green-lt.
215	△	320	Pistachio Green-med.
216	⋮	367	Pistachio Green-dk.

Step Two: Backstitch (one strand)

297	A	743	Yellow-med.
76	B	603	Cranberry
86	C	3608	Plum-vy. lt.
88	D	718	Plum
105	E	209	Lavender-dk.
110	F	208	Lavender-vy. dk.

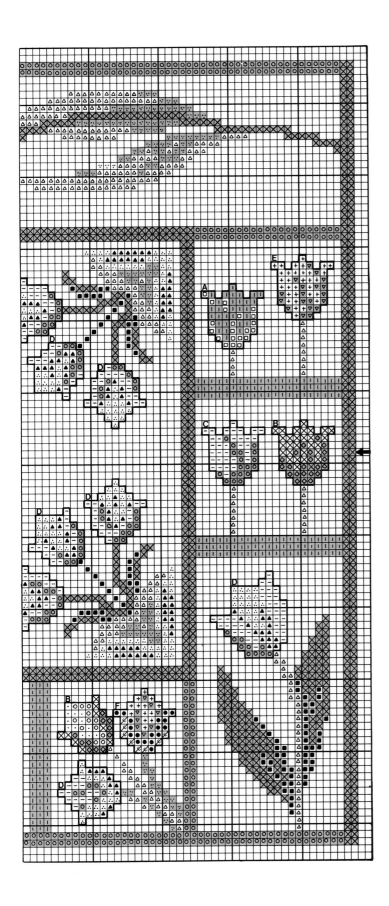

The tulips in the purple frame (see photo) were stitched on white Dublin Linen 25 over one thread. The finished design size is 8⅛″ × 8¾″. The fabric was cut 15″ × 15″.

ANCHOR   DMC (used for sample)

Step One: Cross-stitch (one strand)

301	I	744	Yellow-pale
297	□	743	Yellow-med.
26	·	894	Carnation-vy. lt.
27	O	893	Carnation-lt.
28	X	892	Carnation-med.
35	◇	891	Carnation-dk.
75	–	604	Cranberry-lt.
76	⊙	603	Cranberry
77	∴	602	Cranberry-med.
78	▲	601	Cranberry-dk.
95	+	554	Violet-lt.
98	▽	553	Violet-med.
99	●	552	Violet-dk.
101	⬚	550	Violet-vy. dk.
256	X	704	Chartreuse-bright
239	■	702	Kelly Green
229	△	700	Christmas Green-bright
923	∴	699	Christmas Green

Step Two: Backstitch (one strand)

297	A	743	Yellow-med.
35	B	891	Carnation-dk.
76	C	603	Cranberry
78	D	601	Cranberry-dk.
98	E	553	Violet-med.
101	F	550	Violet-vy. dk.

33

The tulips in the mauve frame (see photo) were stitched on white Dublin Linen 25 over one thread. The finished design size is 8⅜″ × 8¾″. The fabric was cut 15″ × 15″.

The tulips in the navy blue frame (see photo) were stitched on white Dublin Linen 25 over one thread. The finished design size is 8⅜″ × 8¾″. The fabric was cut 15″ × 15″.

ANCHOR   DMC (used for sample)

Step One: Cross-stitch (one strand)

ANCHOR		DMC	
323	I	722	Orange Spice-lt.
324	▣	721	Orange Spice-med.
46	·	321	Christmas Red
47	◉	304	Christmas Red-med.
22	✕	816	Garnet
43	◇	815	Garnet-med.
9	−	352	Coral-lt.
10	○	351	Coral
11	∴	350	Coral-med.
13	▲	349	Coral-dk.
969	+	316	Antique Mauve-med.
970	▽	315	Antique Mauve-dk.
871	●	3041	Antique Violet-med.
70	✗	3685	Mauve-dk.
842	✕	3013	Khaki Green-lt.
844	■	3012	Khaki Green-med.
845	△	3011	Khaki Green-dk.
269	⠿	936	Avocado Green-vy. dk.

Step Two: Backstitch (one strand)

ANCHOR		DMC	
324	A	721	Orange Spice-med.
43	B	815	Garnet-med.
10	C	351	Coral
13	D	349	Coral-dk.
970	E	315	Antique Mauve-dk.
70	F	3685	Mauve-dk.

ANCHOR   DMC (used for sample)

Step One: Cross-stitch (one strand)

ANCHOR		DMC	
886	I	677	Old Gold-vy. lt.
887	▣	3046	Yellow Beige-med.
892	·	225	Shell Pink-vy. lt.
893	○	224	Shell Pink-lt.
894	✕	223	Shell Pink-med.
897	◇	221	Shell Pink-dk.
968	−	778	Antique Mauve-lt.
969	○	316	Antique Mauve-med.
970	∴	315	Antique Mauve-dk.
72	▲	902	Garnet-vy. dk.
869	+	3042	Antique Violet-lt.
871	▽	3041	Antique Violet-med.
100	●	327	Antique Violet-dk.
101	✗	550	Violet-vy. dk.
859	✕	523	Fern Green-lt.
862	■	520	Fern Green-dk.
876	△	502	Blue Green
878	⠿	501	Blue Green-dk.

Step Two: Backstitch (one strand)

ANCHOR		DMC	
901	A	680	Old Gold-dk.
897	B	221	Shell Pink-dk.
969	C	316	Antique Mauve-med.
970	D	315	Antique Mauve-dk.
871	E	3041	Antique Violet-med.
101	F	550	Violet-vy. dk.

"JUNE BRINGS TULIPS
LILIES, ROSES,
FILLS THE CHILDREN'S
HANDS WITH POSIES"
— Sara Coleridge —

𝔉LIGHTS OF FANCY

Stitched on cream Belfast Linen 32 over two threads, the finished design size is 1¾″ × 1¾″. The fabric was cut 5″ × 5″. See suppliers for porcelain boxes.

FABRIC	DESIGN SIZES
Aida 11	2⅝″ × 2¼″
Aida 14	2⅛″ × 1¾″
Aida 18	1⅝″ × 1⅜″
Hardanger 22	1⅜″ × 1⅛″

ANCHOR **DMC (used for sample)**

Step One: Cross-stitch (two strands)

ANCHOR			DMC	
926	·			Ecru
893	−	╱	224	Shell Pink-lt.
894	△		223	Shell Pink-med.
70	∴	╱	3685	Mauve-dk.
859	✕		3052	Gray Green-med.
215	○		320	Pistachio Green-med.
246	■	╱	319	Pistachio Green-vy. dk.
388	◇	╱	3033	Mocha Brown-vy. lt.
903	▼	╱	3032	Mocha Brown-med.
401	●	╱	844	Beaver Gray-ultra dk.

Step Two: Backstitch (one strand)

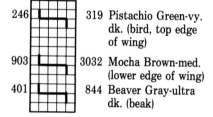

246	319	Pistachio Green-vy. dk. (bird, top edge of wing)
903	3032	Mocha Brown-med. (lower edge of wing)
401	844	Beaver Gray-ultra dk. (beak)

Stitch Count: 29 × 25

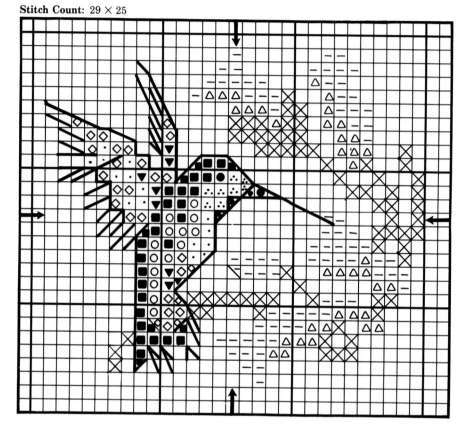

Stitched on cream Belfast Linen 32 over two threads, the finished design size is 1¾″ × 1¾″. The fabric was cut 5″ × 5″. See suppliers for porcelain boxes.

FABRIC | DESIGN SIZES
Aida 11 | 2½″ × 2½″
Aida 14 | 2″ × 1⅞″
Aida 18 | 1½″ × 1½″
Hardanger 22 | 1¼″ × 1¼″

ANCHOR DMC (used for sample)

Step One: Cross-stitch (two strands)

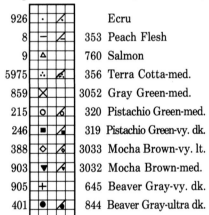

926	·	⁄	Ecru
8	=	⁄	353 Peach Flesh
9	△		760 Salmon
5975	∴	◿	356 Terra Cotta-med.
859	☓		3052 Gray Green-med.
215	○	◿	320 Pistachio Green-med.
246	■	◿	319 Pistachio Green-vy. dk.
388	◇	◿	3033 Mocha Brown-vy. lt.
903	▼	◿	3032 Mocha Brown-med.
905	+		645 Beaver Gray-vy. dk.
401	●	◿	844 Beaver Gray-ultra dk.

Step Two: Backstitch (one strand)

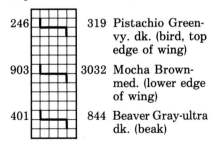

246	319 Pistachio Green-vy. dk. (bird, top edge of wing)
903	3032 Mocha Brown-med. (lower edge of wing)
401	844 Beaver Gray-ultra dk. (beak)

Stitch Count: 28 × 27

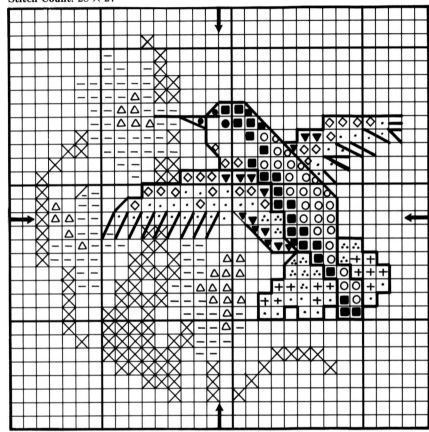

FLORAL PERFUME TRAY

Stitched on sand Dublin Linen 25 over two threads, the finished design size is 9⅞″ × 3⅞″. The fabric was cut 16″ × 10″. See suppliers for wooden tray.

FABRIC	DESIGN SIZES
Aida 11	11¼″ × 4⅜″
Aida 14	8⅞″ × 3⅜″
Aida 18	6⅞″ × 2⅝″
Hardanger 22	5⅝″ × 2⅛″

ANCHOR   DMC (used for sample)

Step One: Cross-stitch (two strands)

293	·	⁄	727 Topaz-vy. lt.
306	F	⁄	725 Topaz
307	+	⁄	783 Christmas Gold
11	□	⁄	351 Coral
13	●	⁄	349 Coral-dk.
42	△	⁄	335 Rose
59	■	⁄	326 Rose-vy. deep
69	○	⁄	3687 Mauve
70	▲	⁄	3685 Mauve-dk.

ANCHOR   FLOWER THREAD
(used for sample; one strand)

255	–	907 Parrot Green-lt.
267	M	470 Avocado Green-lt.
243	∴	988 Forest Green-med.
210	U	562 Jade-med.
878	X	501 Blue Green-dk.

Step Two: Backstitch (one strand)

308		350 Topaz (yellow flowers)
267		470 Avocado Green-lt. (stems on yellow flowers)
878		501 Blue Green-dk. (all else)

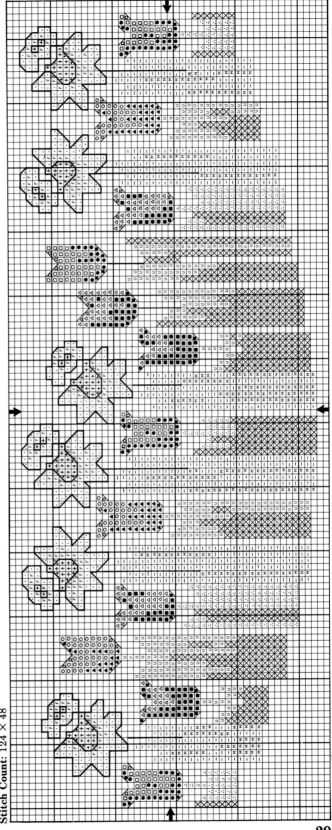

Stitch Count: 124 × 48

BUTTON, BUTTON . . .

Stitched on cream Aida 18 over one thread, the finished design size is 1⅜″ × 1⅜″. The fabric was cut 4″ × 4″. Cover 1½″–wide buttons with designs.

FABRIC	DESIGN SIZES
Aida 11	2⅛″ × 2⅛″
Aida 14	1¾″ × 1¾″
Hardanger 22	1⅛″ × 1⅛″

ANCHOR   DMC (used for sample)

Step One: Cross-stitch (two strands)

886	3047 Yellow Beige-lt.
323	722 Orange Spice-lt.
324	721 Orange Spice-med.
11	3328 Salmon-med.
920	932 Antique Blue-lt.
843	3364 Pine Green
215	320 Pistachio Green-med.
216	367 Pistachio Green-dk.
341	918 Red Copper-dk.
381	3021 Brown Gray-dk.

Step Two: Backstitch (one strand)

382	3371 Black Brown

Stitch Count: 24 × 24

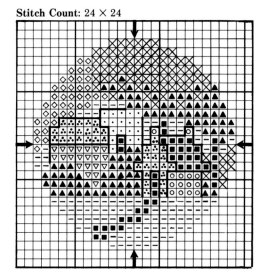

Stitch Count: 24 × 24

Stitch Count: 24 × 24

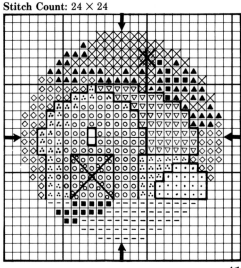

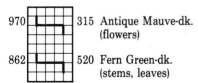OSIES IN A BASKET

MATERIALS

Completed cross-stitch on mint parfait Soft Touch 14
1¼ yards of mauve-striped fabric; matching thread
2 yards of small cording
One 17½″ × 17½″ square of mauve fabric

All seam allowances are ¼″.

1 Trim the design piece to a 16″ × 16″ square with center of each row of design 2″ from left and bottom edges.

2 Cut one 16″ and one 17½″ square of striped fabric.

Also cut a 1″-wide bias, piecing as needed, to equal two yards. Make two yards of corded piping.

3 Stitch piping to design piece, right sides together, rounding corners slightly. With right sides of design piece and 16″ square of striped fabric together, stitch on stitching line of piping, leaving a small opening. Clip corners. Turn. Slipstitch the opening closed.

4 For the liner, stitch the 17½″ square mauve and striped pieces with right sides together, leaving a small opening. Clip corners. Turn. Slipstitch the opening closed.

Stitched on mint parfait Soft Touch 14 over one thread, the finished design size is 4¾″ × 5¼″. The fabric was cut 18″ × 18″. The center of each row is 2″ from the bottom and side edges.

FABRIC	DESIGN SIZES
Aida 11	6″ × 6⅝″
Aida 14	4¾″ × 5¼″
Aida 18	3⅝″ × 4″
Hardanger 22	3″ × 3⅜″

ANCHOR   DMC (used for sample)

Step One: Cross-stitch (two strands)

968	–	778	Antique Mauve-lt.
969	o	316	Antique Mauve-med.
970	▲	315	Antique Mauve-dk.
859	✕	522	Fern Green

Step Two: Backstitch (one strand)

970		315	Antique Mauve-dk. (flowers)
862		520	Fern Green-dk. (stems, leaves)

Stitch Count: 66 × 73

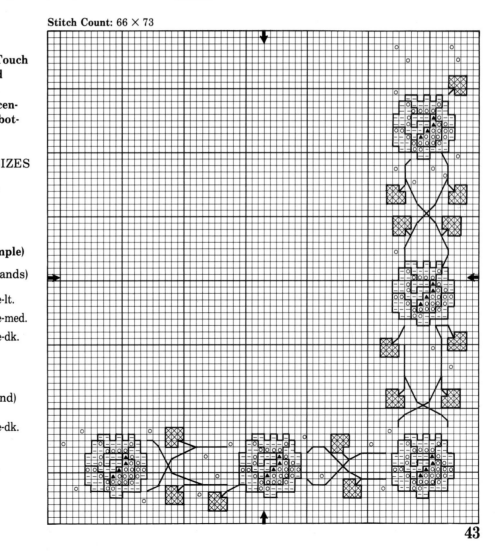

COLORS OF SPRING

Stitched on cream Hardanger 22 over two threads, the finished design size is 6″ × 5⅛″. The fabric was cut 10″ × 10″. See suppliers for box.

FABRIC	DESIGN SIZES
Aida 11	6″ × 5⅛″
Aida 14	4¾″ × 4⅛″
Aida 18	3⅝″ × 3⅛″
Hardanger 22	3″ × 2⅝″

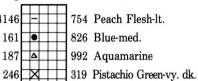

ANCHOR   DMC (used for sample)

Step One: Cross-stitch (three strands)

4146	−	754 Peach Flesh-lt.
161	●	826 Blue-med.
187	△	992 Aquamarine
246	✕	319 Pistachio Green-vy. dk.
341	∴	918 Red Copper-dk.

Step Two: Backstitch (one strand)

| 161 | | 826 Blue-med. (bird's beaks) |
| 246 | | 319 Pistachio Green-vy. dk. (stems) |

Stitch Count: 66 × 56

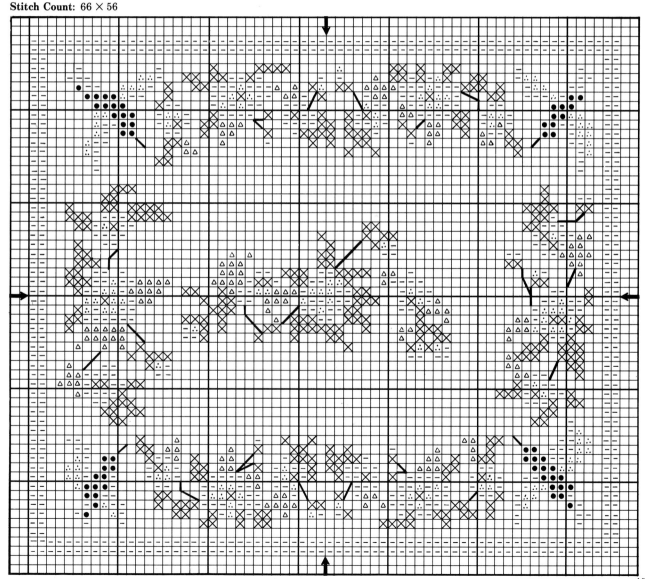

DAMASK TABLE RUNNER

Stitched on cream Shonfels Damask 11 over one thread, the finished design size is 3⅜" × 3⅜". The fabric was cut 1 pattern × 6 patterns with ½ pattern on each side. See suppliers for beads and silk ribbons.

FABRIC	DESIGN SIZES
Aida 11	3⅜" × 3⅜"
Aida 14	2⅝" × 2⅝"
Aida 18	2" × 2"
Hardanger 22	1⅝" × 1⅝"

ANCHOR   DMC (used for sample)

Step One: Cross-stitch (two strands)

301	·	744 Yellow-pale
301	N	744 Yellow-pale (bead sewn over x-stitch)
308	+	782 Topaz-med.
308	∴	782 Topaz-med. (bead sewn over x-stitch)
66	▫	3688 Mauve-med. (bead sewn over x-stitch)
70	◀	3685 Mauve-dk. (bead sewn over x-stitch)
120	○	794 Cornflower Blue-lt.
120	I	794 Cornflower Blue-lt. (bead sewn over x-stitch)
940	■	792 Cornflower Blue-dk.
940	●	792 Cornflower Blue-dk. (bead sewn over x-stitch)
265	◁	3348 Yellow Green-lt.
257	✕	3346 Hunter Green

Step Two: Backstitch (one strand)

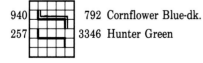

940	792 Cornflower Blue-dk.
257	3346 Hunter Green

Step Three: Beads (sewn over x-stitch)

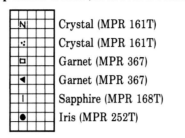

N	Crystal (MPR 161T)
∴	Crystal (MPR 161T)
▫	Garnet (MPR 367)
◀	Garnet (MPR 367)
I	Sapphire (MPR 168T)
●	Iris (MPR 252T)

Step Four: Silk Ribbons

Stitch Count: 37 × 37

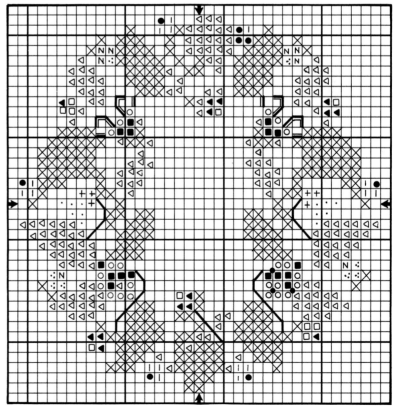

MATERIALS

Completed cross-stitch on cream Shonfels Damask; matching thread
1 ball #20 DMC yellow Cebelia cotton crochet thread
Size 10 steel crochet hook

1 Crochet the edging.

A. Chain 153.

Row 1: Work 1 sc in 9th ch from hook, * ch 5. Skip 3 ch, sc in next ch; repeat from * to end of row. Ch 5, turn.

Row 2: * Sc in center ch of ch-5 loop, ch 5; repeat from *, ending in 6th ch of turning ch. Ch 5, turn.

Row 3: * Sc in center ch of ch-5 loop, ch 5; repeat from * to end of row. Ch 5, turn.

Repeat row 3 ten times, making a total of 13 rows. To finish with a straight edge, ch 3 between each sc on row 14.

B. Row 1 of ring border: * ch 21, join on the right to the 3rd stitch to form ring; 23 sc in ring. 1 sc in ch preceding the stitch which closed the ring. Ch 2, attach to straight edge (skipping ch 3 and sc), sc across next 12 stitches. Repeat from * across straight edge (10 rings). Tie off.

Row 2: * 1 sc in 4th sc of 23 sc in ring. # Ch 1, skip one sc of ring then sc in next; repeat from # to total 8 loops. Ch 4, 1 sc in 6th and 7th of the 12 chain stitches, ch 4; repeat from *.

Row 3: 1 sc in 1st loop of chain stitches, ch 3, 1 sc in 2nd loop. * # Ch 4 and 1 sc in next loop; repeat from # to total 5 loops. Ch 3, 1 sc in last loop, ch 2, 1 sc in 1st loop of the next ring, ch 2. Connect to last loop of previous ring. Ch 1, sc in next loop of new ring; repeat from *.

C. Repeat for second edging.

2 Trim Damask to size desired.

3 Stitch ¼" hem by hand on all edges; press.

4 Slipstitch crocheted edging to fold line at each end of runner.

" Blossom by blossom
the spring begins. "
— *Algernon C. Swinburne* —

MAGNIFICENT BIRD

Stitched on cream Aida 14 over one thread, the finished design size is 10¼″ × 10⅛″. The fabric was cut 17″ × 17″.

FABRIC	DESIGN SIZES
Aida 11	13″ × 12⅞″
Aida 18	8″ × 7⅞″
Hardanger 22	6½″ × 6⅜″

ANCHOR   DMC (used for sample)

Step One: Cross-stitch (two strands)

Anchor	Symbol	DMC	Color
386	•	746	Off White
891	◇	676	Old Gold-lt.
890	⌐	729	Old Gold-med.
306	G	783	Christmas Gold
9	✗	760	Salmon
11	U	3328	Salmon-med.
13	F	347	Salmon-dk.
74	I	3354	Dusty Rose-lt.
27	▽	899	Rose-med.
42	✕	335	Rose
130	S	809	Delft
131	M	798	Delft-dk.
203	J	954	Nile Green
209	K	913	Nile Green-med.
205	E	911	Emerald Green-med.
186	O	993	Aquamarine-lt.
187	⋮	992	Aquamarine
266	•	3347	Yellow Green-med.

Stitch Count: 143 × 141

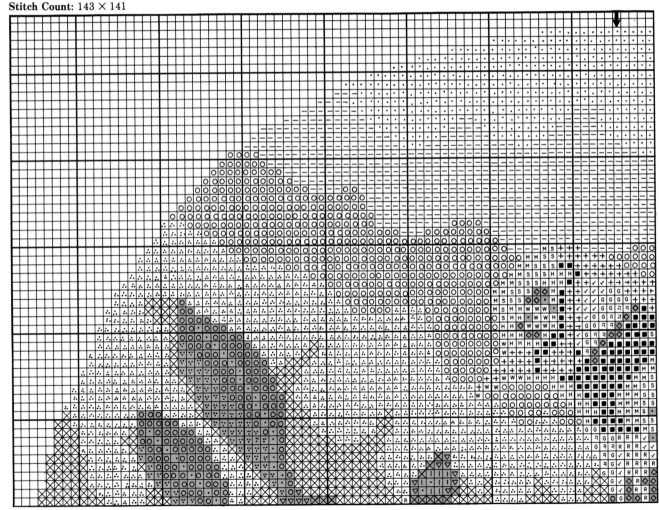

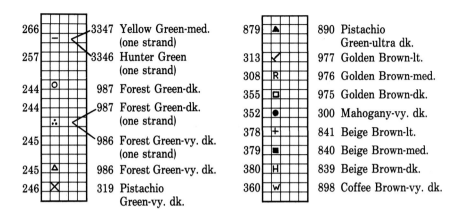

266	3347	Yellow Green-med. (one strand)
257	3346	Hunter Green (one strand)
244	987	Forest Green-dk.
244	987	Forest Green-dk. (one strand)
245	986	Forest Green-vy. dk. (one strand)
245	986	Forest Green-vy. dk.
246	319	Pistachio Green-vy. dk.
879	890	Pistachio Green-ultra dk.
313	977	Golden Brown-lt.
308	976	Golden Brown-med.
355	975	Golden Brown-dk.
352	300	Mahogany-vy. dk.
378	841	Beige Brown-lt.
379	840	Beige Brown-med.
380	839	Beige Brown-dk.
360	898	Coffee Brown-vy. dk.

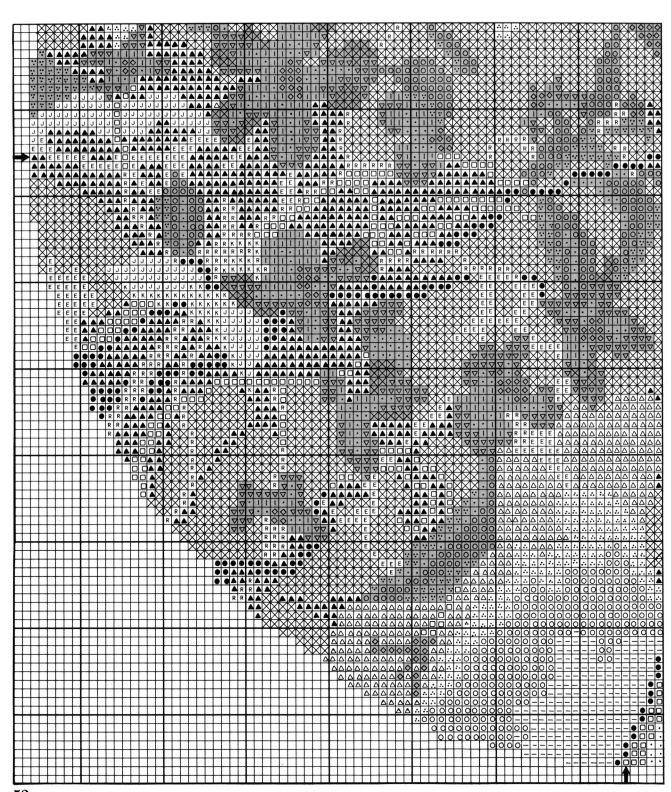

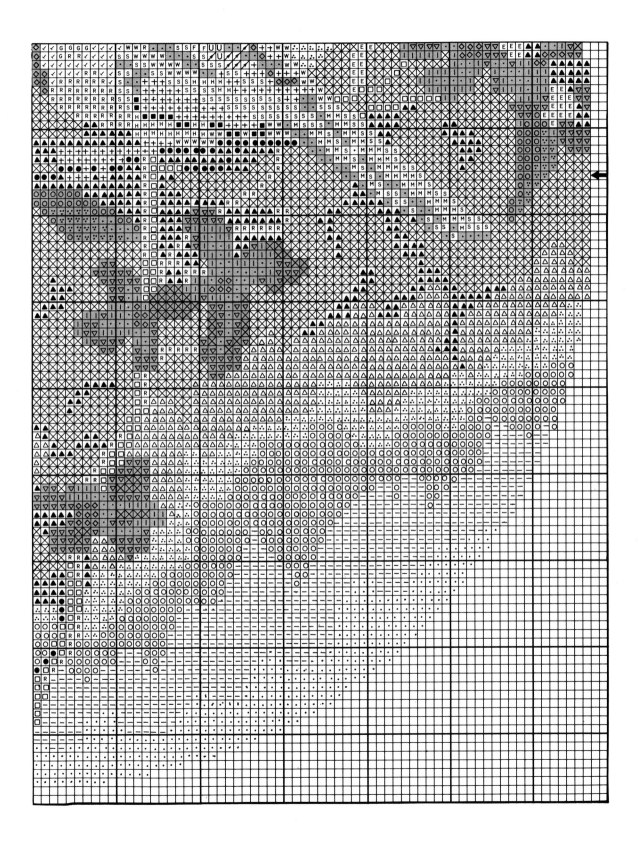

SUMMER

ROSES IN BLOOM

Stitched on cream Belfast Linen 32 over two threads, the finished design size for #1 is ⅝″ × 6″, #2 is ¾″ × 6″, #3 is 1¼″ × 6″, #4 is 2″ × 6″, #5 is 2¾″ × 6″. The fabric was cut 11″ × 14″ for all designs.

FABRIC	DESIGN SIZES #1	DESIGN SIZES #2
Aida 11	⅞″ X 8¾″	1⅛″ X 8¾″
Aida 14	¾″ X 6⅞″	⅞″ X 6⅞″
Aida 18	½″ X 5⅜″	¾″ X 5⅜″
Hardanger 22	½″ X 4⅜″	⅝″ X 4⅜″

FABRIC	DESIGN SIZES #3	DESIGN SIZES #4
Aida 11	1⅞″ X 8¾″	3″ X 8¾″
Aida 14	1½″ X 6⅞″	2¼″ X 6⅞″
Aida 18	1⅛″ X 5⅜″	1¾″ X 5⅜″
Hardanger 22	1″ X 4⅜″	1½″ X 4⅜″

FABRIC	DESIGN SIZES #5
Aida 11	4″ X 8¾″
Aida 14	3⅛″ X 6⅞″
Aida 18	2⅜″ X 5⅜″
Hardanger 22	2″ X 4⅜″

ANCHOR DMC (used for sample)

Step One: Cross-stitch (two strands)

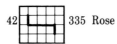

ANCHOR	Symbol	DMC
301	·	744 Yellow-pale (one strand)
8	·	353 Peach Flesh (one strand)
10	–	352 Coral-lt.
10	☒	352 Coral-lt. (one strand)
42	☒	335 Rose (one strand)
42	●	335 Rose
255	△	907 Parrot Green-lt. (one strand)
242	△	989 Forest Green (one strand)
243	∴	988 Forest Green-med.
244	■	987 Forest Green-dk. (one strand)
246	■	319 Pistachio Green-vy. dk. (one strand)

Step Two: Backstitch (one strand)

ANCHOR	DMC
42	335 Rose

#1 Stitch Count: 10 × 96

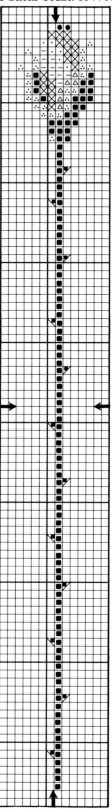

#2 Stitch Count: 13 × 96   #3 Stitch Count: 21 × 96   #4 Stitch Count: 32 × 96

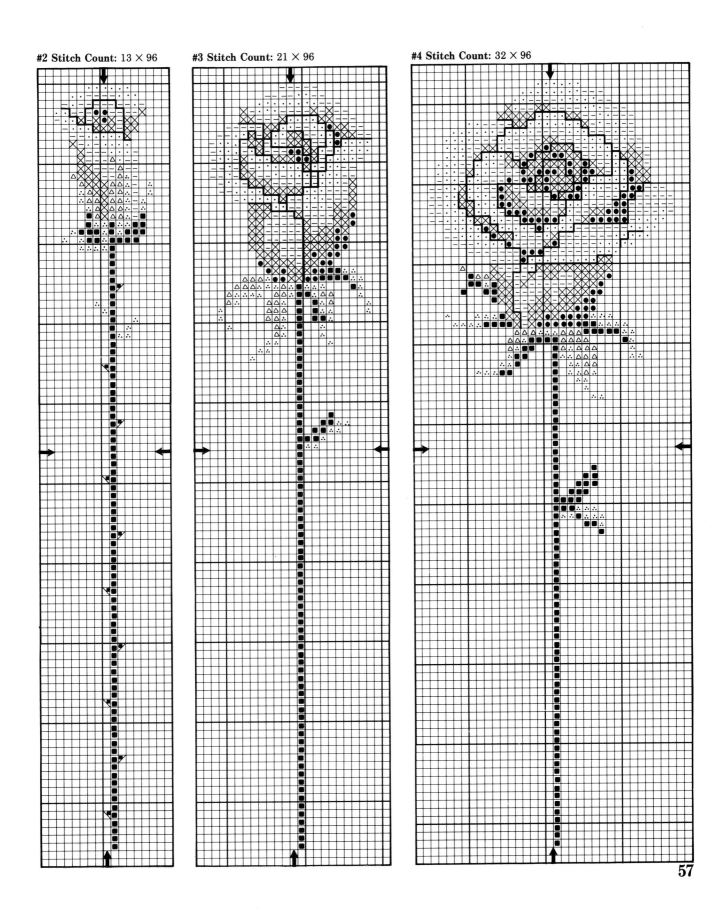

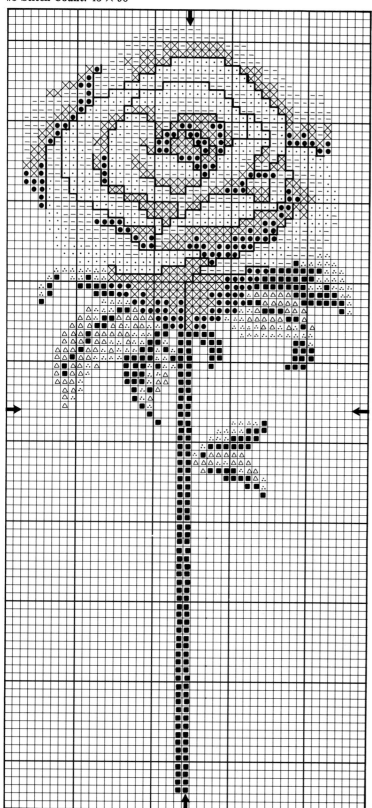

" . . . A N D   I   W I L L   M A K E
T H E E   B E D S   O F   R O S E S
A N D   A   T H O U S A N D
F R A G R A N T   P O S I E S . "

— Christopher Marlowe —

TEA-WASHED TWINS

Stitched on cream Dublin Linen 25 over two threads, the finished design size for one motif is 3⅞" × 1¾". The fabric was cut 24" × 15". The vertical center of the design should be 4" from the bottom edge of the fabric. The heavy black lines on the graph show the placement for the repeats.

FABRIC	DESIGN SIZES
Aida 11	4½" × 2"
Aida 14	3½" × 1⅝"
Aida 18	2¾" × 1¼"
Hardanger 22	2¼" × 1"

ANCHOR   DMC (used for sample)

Step One: Cross-stitch (two strands)

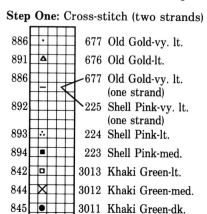

886	·	677 Old Gold-vy. lt.
891	△	676 Old Gold-lt.
886	—	677 Old Gold-vy. lt. (one strand)
892		225 Shell Pink-vy. lt. (one strand)
893	∴	224 Shell Pink-lt.
894	■	223 Shell Pink-med.
842	▫	3013 Khaki Green-lt.
844	✕	3012 Khaki Green-med.
845	●	3011 Khaki Green-dk.

Step Two: Backstitch (one strand)

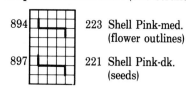

| 894 | 223 Shell Pink-med. (flower outlines) |
| 897 | 221 Shell Pink-dk. (seeds) |

Step Three: French knots (one strand)

| 897 | ● | 221 Shell Pink-dk. |

Stitch Count: 49 × 22 (one motif)

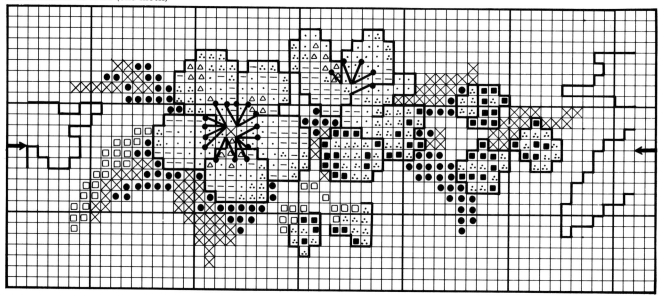

Stitched on cream Dublin Linen 25 over two threads, the finished design size for one motif is 2½" × 1¼". The fabric was cut 24" × 15". The vertical center of the design should be 4" from the bottom edge of the fabric. The heavy black lines on the graph show the placement for the repeats.

FABRIC	DESIGN SIZES
Aida 11	3" × 1½"
Aida 14	2¼" × 1⅛"
Aida 18	1¾" × ⅞"
Hardanger 22	1½" × ¾"

ANCHOR   DMC (used for sample)

Step One: Cross-stitch (two strands)

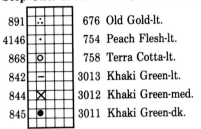

891	∴	676 Old Gold-lt.
4146	·	754 Peach Flesh-lt.
868	o	758 Terra Cotta-lt.
842	−	3013 Khaki Green-lt.
844	X	3012 Khaki Green-med.
845	●	3011 Khaki Green-dk.

Step Two: Backstitch (one strand)

5975   356 Terra Cotta-med.

Stitch Count: 32 × 16 (one motif)

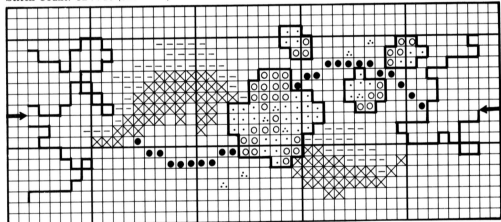

"THE SEASONS BRING THE FLOWERS AGAIN."
— Alfred Lord Tennyson —

61

MATERIALS for one doll body

¼ **yard of tea-washed* muslin; matching thread**
Stuffing
One skein tan yarn for hair
Large-eyed needle
Dark brown embroidery floss for eyes
Dressmakers' pen
Tracing paper for patterns

All seam allowances are ¼".

1 Make patterns for head/body, arm, leg and foot, transferring all information. From tea-washed muslin, cut body pieces as indicated on patterns.

2 With right sides together, stitch two arm pieces, leaving an opening as indicated on pattern. Clip seam allowance at thumb. Turn. Stuff one arm firmly to within ½" of top. Stitch the top edge. Repeat for second arm.

3 With right sides together, stitch two leg pieces. Clip corners. Turn. Stuff one leg firmly to within ½" of top. Stitch the top edge. Repeat for second leg.

4 Pin arms to right side of one body piece with hands toward center of body; see pattern. With right sides of two body pieces together and with arms sandwiched between, stitch head and sides, leaving bottom edge open. Turn.

5 Pin legs to right side of body front; see pattern. Stitch.

6 Stuff body firmly. Turn seam allowance at bottom edge inside; slipstitch.

7 Transfer hairline from pattern to doll head. Also draw a line down center of back of head, ending ½" above neck.

For hair on back of head, use 14" lengths of yarn. Thread one length onto large-eyed needle and stitch in place; see diagram. Repeat with stitches close together until hairline is covered.

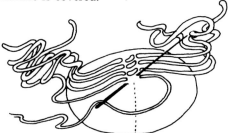

For bangs, use 16" lengths of yarn. Fold each length in half. At center of forehead, place yarn on head with folded end toward face. With matching thread, tack yarn into place, leaving 1" of loop for bangs; see diagram. Complete one half of head, then second half.
Braid hair on each side of head. Tie ends of braid with short lengths of yarn. Tack top of braids to each side of head.

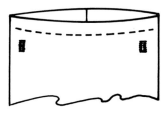

8 Using two strands of floss, make French knots for eyes, wrapping floss around needle once.

MATERIALS for dress

Completed cross-stitch on cream Dublin Linen 25, tea-washed*; matching thread
¾ yard of ⅜"-wide cream satin ribbon

All seam allowances are ¼".

1 Cut tea-washed linen 22" × 13½" with bottom row of stitching 2¼" from one 22" edge.

2 Fold dress right sides together to measure 11½" wide. Stitch the center back seam.

3 Fold ½" double to wrong side for hem. Slipstitch.

4 To make casing at neck, fold over ½". Stitch. Carefully cut threads in center back seam of casing.

5 Make two ¾"-long buttonholes near the top edge of dress for arm holes; see diagram.

6 Thread the ribbon through the casing. Place the dress on the doll. Gather the neckline to fit the doll. Tie ribbon in a knot, then a bow.

* **Tea-washing—Soak fabric in a container of strong, dark tea until fabric reaches desired shade of brown. The fabric will be unevenly dyed and will appear lighter in color when dry.**

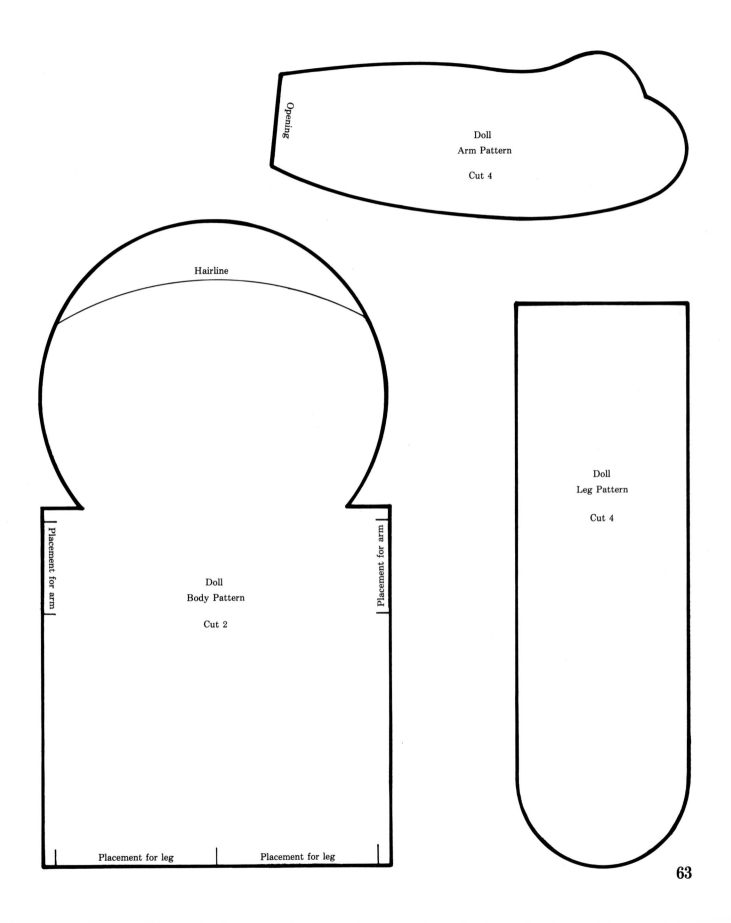

Opening

Doll
Arm Pattern

Cut 4

Hairline

Doll
Body Pattern

Cut 2

Placement for arm

Placement for arm

Placement for leg

Placement for leg

Doll
Leg Pattern

Cut 4

63

THREE CLASSIC PILLOWS

Stitched on white Jobelan 28 over two threads, the finished design size is 8⅜″ × 3⅞″. The fabric was cut 17″ × 23″.

FABRIC	DESIGN SIZES
Aida 11	10¾″ × 5″
Aida 14	8⅜″ × 3⅞″
Aida 18	6½″ × 3″
Hardanger 22	5⅜″ × 2½″

ANCHOR   DMC (used for sample)

Step One: Cross-stitch (two strands)

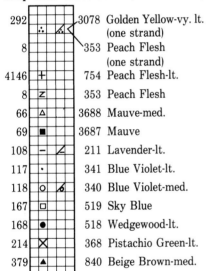

292		3078	Golden Yellow-vy. lt. (one strand)
8		353	Peach Flesh (one strand)
4146	+	754	Peach Flesh-lt.
8	Z	353	Peach Flesh
66	△	3688	Mauve-med.
69	■	3687	Mauve
108	–	211	Lavender-lt.
117	·	341	Blue Violet-lt.
118	○	340	Blue Violet-med.
167	□	519	Sky Blue
168	●	518	Wedgewood-lt.
214	✕	368	Pistachio Green-lt.
379	▲	840	Beige Brown-med.

Step Two: Backstitch (one strand)

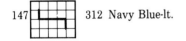

147   312 Navy Blue-lt.

Step Three: French Knots (one strand)

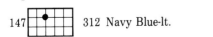

147   312 Navy Blue-lt.

Stitch Count: 118 × 55 (bluebird)

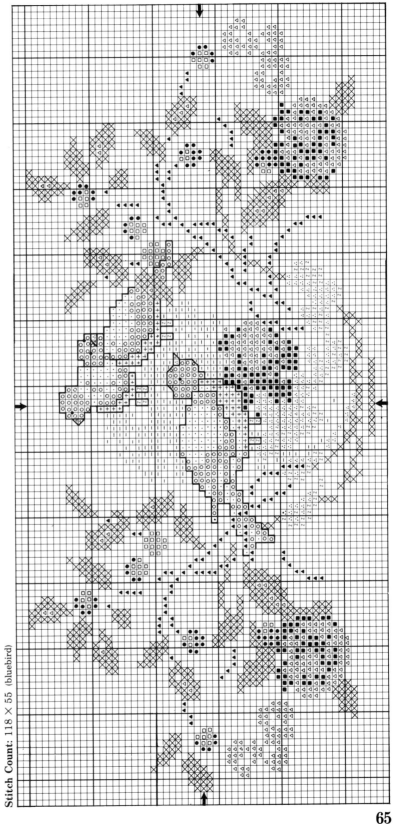

Stitched on white Jobelan 28 over
two threads, the finished design
size is 7⅜" × 4". The fabric was
cut 19" × 21".

FABRIC	DESIGN SIZES
Aida 11	9½" × 5⅛"
Aida 14	7⅜" × 4"
Aida 18	5¾" × 3⅛"
Hardanger 22	4¾" × 2½"

ANCHOR   DMC (used for sample)

Step One: Cross-stitch (two strands)

300	−		745	Yellow-lt. pale
8	+		353	Peach Flesh
28	E		3706	Melon-med.
66	•	╱	3688	Mauve-med.
69	■		3687	Mauve
117	∴		341	Blue Violet-lt.
118	△		340	Blue Violet-med.
119	Z		333	Blue Violet-dk.
214	X		368	Pistachio Green-lt.
215	I		320	Pistachio Green-med.
216	O		367	Pistachio Green-dk.
246	▲		319	Pistachio Green-vy. dk.
882	□	◢	407	Sportsman Flesh-dk.
378	N	◣	841	Beige Brown-lt.
380	●	◢	839	Beige Brown-dk.

Step Two: Backstitch (one strand)

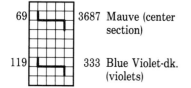

69		3687	Mauve (center section)
119		333	Blue Violet-dk. (violets)

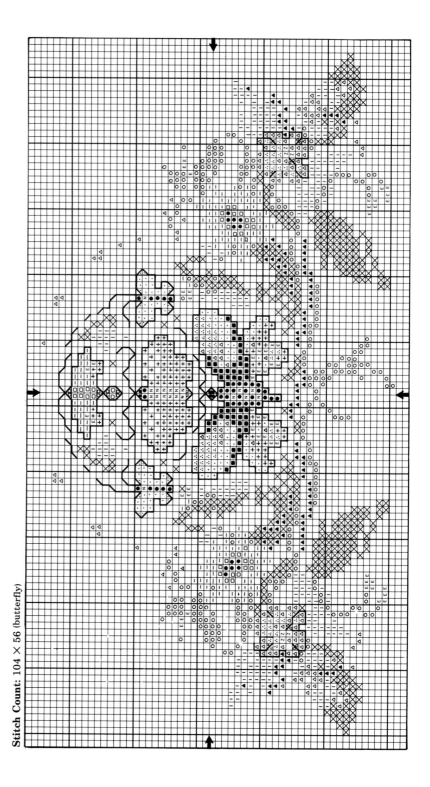

Stitch Count: 104 × 56 (butterfly)

Stitched on white Jobelan 28 over two threads, the finished design size is 8¼″ × 4⅛″. The fabric was cut 20″ × 23″. The heavy black lines on the graph show the placement for the repeats.

FABRIC	DESIGN SIZES
Aida 11	10½″ × 5¼″
Aida 14	8¼″ × 4⅛″
Aida 18	6½″ × 3¼″
Hardanger 22	5¼″ × 2⅝″

ANCHOR   DMC (used for sample)

Step One: Cross-stitch (two strands)

292	=	3078	Golden Yellow-vy. lt.
8	+	353	Peach Flesh
49	△	3689	Mauve-lt.
66	•	3688	Mauve-med.
69	■	3687	Mauve
117	o	341	Blue Violet-lt.
118	∴	340	Blue Violet-med.
167	□	519	Sky Blue
168	●	518	Wedgewood-lt.
265	X	3348	Yellow Green-lt.
214	z	368	Pistachio Green-lt.
215	▲	320	Pistachio Green-med.

Step Two: Backstitch (one strand)

890	⌐	729	Old Gold-med. (inside yellow flowers)
215	L	320	Pistachio Green-med. (veins in leaves)

Stitch Count: 116 × 58 (bouquets-in-a-row)

MATERIALS for bluebird design

Completed cross-stitch on white Belfast Linen 32; matching thread
¼ yard of unstitched white Belfast Linen 32
⅜ yard of white satin
2½ yards of ¼″-wide cording
1¼ yards of 4″-wide white flat eyelet
Two 1½″-wide buttons to cover
Stuffing

All seam allowances are ¼″.

1 Cut design piece 9″ × 19½″ with design centered horizontally. Cut two 3½″ × 19½″ pieces for insets and two 2½″ × 19½″ pieces for ends from unstitched linen. From satin, cut 1¼″-wide bias, piecing as needed, to equal 2¼ yards. Make 2¼ yards of corded piping. Also cover two buttons with satin.

2 Stitch cording to one long edge of each 2½″-wide strip for inset. Matching long edges, stitch 3½″-wide strips for ends to 2½″-wide strips, stitching on stitching line of piping. Fold inset/end pieces in half with right sides together, matching short edges. Stitch closed. Turn.

3 Cut two 19½″ pieces of eyelet. Fold with right sides together, matching short edges. Stitch ends of each together. Turn. Slide the eyelet over the right side of the inset/end piece with eyelet right side up. Pin raw edges together.

4 Stitch cording to both 19½″ edges of design piece. Place design piece over one eyelet piece, right sides together, matching seams. Stitch on stitching line of cording. Repeat on opposite end of design piece.

5 Fold under ⅛″ on ends. Stitch strong gathering thread near fold. On one end, gather tightly and secure threads. Stuff pillow firmly. Gather second end and secure threads. Sew buttons over gathered ends.

MATERIALS for butterfly design

Completed cross-stitch on white Belfast Linen 32; matching thread
⅛ yard of unstitched white Belfast Linen 32
¼ yard of white satin
1¼ yards of ¼″-wide cording
2½ yards of 5½″-wide flat eyelet
Two 1½″-wide buttons to cover
Stuffing

1 Cut design piece 15½″ × 19½″ with the designs centered. Cut two 3½″ × 19½″ pieces from unstitched linen for ends. From satin, cut 1¼″-wide bias, piecing as needed, to equal 40″. Make 40″ of corded piping.

68

Also cover two buttons with satin. Cut eyelet into two equal pieces.

2 Stitch cording to both 19½″ edges of design piece. Fold design piece in half with right sides together, matching long edges. Stitch closed. Turn. Stitch gathering threads on raw edge of eyelet strips. Gather to 19½″. Place eyelet on ends of design piece, aligning raw edges. Stitch on stitching line of piping.

3 Stitch ends of one eyelet strip together. Repeat with second strip.

4 Stitch ends together of one 3½″ × 19½″ linen piece. Repeat with second piece. Match pieces to each end of design piece, aligning seams. Stitch on stitching line of piping.

5 Fold under ⅛″ on ends. Stitch strong gathering thread near fold. On one end, gather tightly and secure threads. Stuff pillow firmly. Gather second end and secure threads. Sew buttons over gathered ends.

MATERIALS for bouquets-in-a-row design

Completed cross-stitch on white Belfast Linen 32; matching thread
⅛ yard of unstitched white Belfast Linen 32
¼ yard of white satin
1¼ yards of ¼″-wide cording
Two 1½″-wide buttons to cover
Stuffing

1 Cut design piece 17″ × 19½″ with the design centered horizontally. Cut two 3½″ × 19½″ pieces from unstitched linen for ends. From satin, cut 1¼″-wide bias, piecing as needed, to equal 40″. Make 40″ of corded piping. Also cover two buttons with satin.

2 Stitch cording to both 19½″ edges of design piece. Then match the 3½″ × 19½″ pieces to each end. Stitch a stitching line of piping.

3 Fold design piece in half with right sides together, matching long edges. Stitch closed. Turn.

4 Fold under ⅛″ on ends. Stitch strong gathering thread near fold. On one end, gather tightly and secure threads. Stuff pillow firmly. Gather second end and secure threads. Sew buttons over gathered ends.

OSEBUD TABLE RUNNER

Stitched on white Hardanger 22 over two threads, the finished design size for #1 is 14⅛″ × 2⅛″; #2 is 13⅞″ × 2¼″. The fabric was cut 16″ × 67″. The center of #1 is 18″ from the narrow ends; the center of #2 is 8″ from the narrow ends. See suppliers for beads.

FABRIC	DESIGN SIZES #1	DESIGN SIZES #2
Aida 11	14⅛″ × 2⅛″	13⅞″ × 2¼″
Aida 14	11⅛″ × 1¾″	10⅞″ × 1¾″
Aida 18	8⅝″ × 1⅜″	8½″ × 1⅜″
Hardanger 22	7⅛″ × 1⅛″	6⅞″ × 1⅛″

ANCHOR   DMC (used for sample)

Step One: Cross-stitch (three strands)

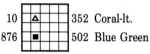

10   352 Coral-lt.

876   502 Blue Green

Step Two: Backstitch (one strand)

876   502 Blue Green

Step Three: Beadwork

Christmas Red (MPR 165T)

#1 Stitch Count: 156 × 24

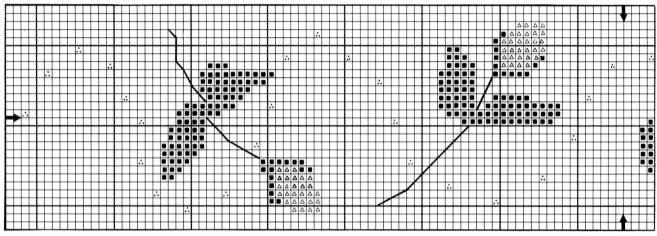

#2 Stitch Count: 152 × 25

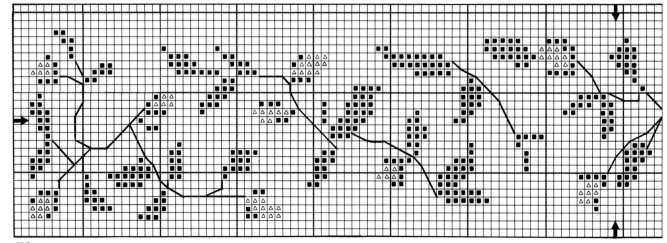

MATERIALS

Completed cross-stitch on white Hardanger 22;
   matching thread
2¾ yards of ⅜"–wide flat white lace
3 yards of ¼"–wide flat white lace
1 yard of ½"–wide flat white lace
½ yard of ⅛"–wide flat white lace
Dressmakers' pen

1 Mark lines on each end of table runner as indicated on diagram. Stitch a narrow hem across each end. Attach lace; see diagram.

2 Stitch a narrow hem on each side, securing lace ends. Stitch ⅜"–wide lace over hem at each end of stitching, making a box.

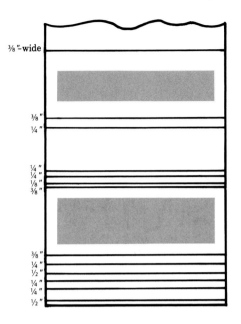

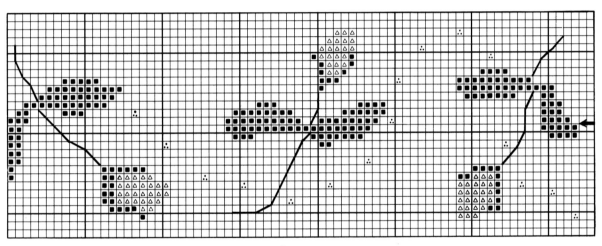

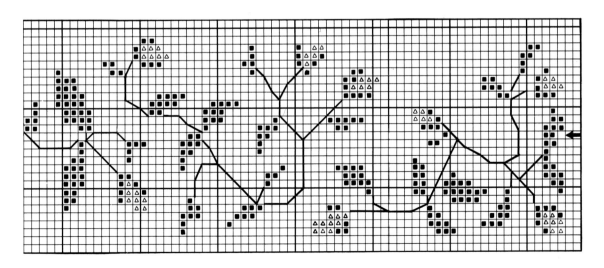

71

SIX EXQUISITE LOCKETS

Stitched on white Belfast Linen 32 over one thread, the finished design size is ¾″ × ⅞″. The fabric was cut 3″ × 3″. See suppliers for lockets.

FABRIC	DESIGN SIZES
Aida 11	2⅛″ × 2½″
Aida 14	1⅝″ × 1⅞″
Aida 18	1¼″ × 1½″
Hardanger 22	1″ × 1¼″

ANCHOR   DMC (used for sample)

Step One: Cross-stitch (one strand)

301		744 Yellow-pale
366	–	951 Sportsman Flesh-vy. lt.
8	O	353 Peach Flesh-vy. lt.
9	▲	760 Salmon
266	△	471 Avocado Green-vy. lt.
257	✕	3346 Hunter Green
246	●	986 Forest Green-vy. dk.

Step Two: Backstitch (one strand)

9		760 Salmon

Stitched on white Belfast Linen 32 over one thread, the finished design size is ½″ × ¾″. The fabric was cut 3″ × 3″. See suppliers for lockets.

FABRIC	DESIGN SIZES
Aida 11	1½″ × 2¼″
Aida 14	1¼″ × 1¾″
Aida 18	1″ × 1⅜″
Hardanger 22	¾″ × 1⅛″

ANCHOR   DMC (used for sample)

Step One: Cross-stitch (one strand)

292		3078 Golden Yellow-vy. lt.
892		225 Shell Pink-vy. lt.
893	O	224 Shell Pink-lt.
894	▲	223 Shell Pink-med.
858	▫	524 Fern Green-vy. lt.
859	✕	522 Fern Green

Step Two: Backstitch (one strand)

894		223 Shell Pink-med.

Stitched on white Belfast Linen 32 over one thread, the finished design size is ⅝″ × ⅝″. The fabric was cut 3″ × 3″. See suppliers for lockets.

FABRIC	DESIGN SIZES
Aida 11	1⅞″ × 2″
Aida 14	1½″ × 1⅝″
Aida 18	1⅛″ × 1¼″
Hardanger 22	1″ × 1″

ANCHOR   DMC (used for sample)

Step One: Cross-stitch (one strand)

886		677 Old Gold-vy. lt.
66	–	3688 Mauve-med.
69	△	3687 Mauve
95	●	554 Violet-lt.
213	▫	504 Blue Green-lt.
215	✕	320 Pistachio Green-med.

Stitch Count: 23 × 27

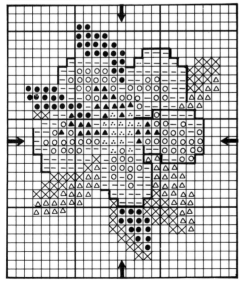

Stitch Count: 17 × 25

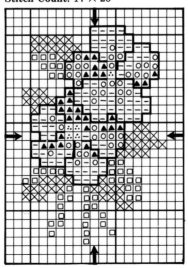

Stitch Count: 21 × 22

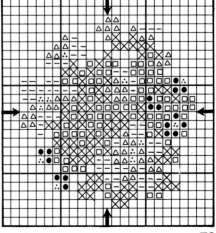

Stitched on white Belfast Linen 32 over one thread, the finished design size is ⅝″ × ⅞″. The fabric was cut 3″ × 3″. See suppliers for lockets.

FABRIC	DESIGN SIZES
Aida 11	1⅞″ × 2⅜″
Aida 14	1⅜″ × 1⅞″
Aida 18	1⅛″ × 1½″
Hardanger 22	⅞″ × 1⅛″

ANCHOR   DMC (used for sample)

Step One: Cross-stitch (one strand)

292	3078	Golden Yellow-vy. lt.
49	3689	Mauve-lt.
117	341	Blue Violet-lt.
118	340	Blue Violet-med.
210	562	Jade-med.

Step Two: Backstitch (one strand)

| 119 | 333 | Blue Violet-dk. |

Stitched on white Belfast Linen 32 over one thread, the finished design size is ¾″ × ¾″. The fabric was cut 3″ × 3″. See suppliers for lockets.

FABRIC	DESIGN SIZES
Aida 11	2⅛″ × 2⅛″
Aida 14	1⅝″ × 1¾″
Aida 18	1¼″ × 1⅜″
Hardanger 22	1″ × 1⅛″

ANCHOR   DMC (used for sample)

Step One: Cross-stitch (one strand)

292	3078	Golden Yellow-vy. lt.
85	3609	Plum-ultra lt.
95	554	Violet-lt.
110	208	Lavender-vy. dk.
214	368	Pistachio Green-lt.
215	320	Pistachio Green-med.

Step Two: Backstitch (one strand)

| 110 | 208 | Lavender-vy. dk. |

Stitched on white Belfast Linen 32 over one thread, the finished design size is ½″ × ⅝″. The fabric was cut 3″ × 3″. See suppliers for lockets.

FABRIC	DESIGN SIZES
Aida 11	1¼″ × 1¾″
Aida 14	1″ × 1⅜″
Aida 18	¾″ × 1″
Hardanger 22	⅝″ × ⅞″

ANCHOR   DMC (used for sample)

Step One: Cross-stitch (one strand)

292	3078	Golden Yellow-vy. lt.
108	211	Lavender-lt.
105	209	Lavender-dk.
110	208	Lavender-vy. dk.
843	3364	Pine Green
861	3363	Pine Green-med.

Stitch Count: 20 × 26

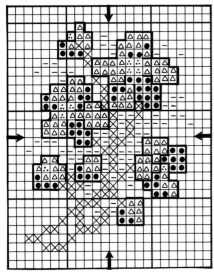

Stitch Count: 23 × 24

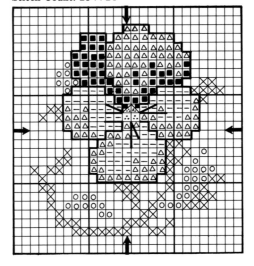

Stitch Count: 14 × 19

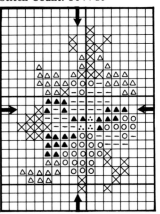

PILLOW, POCKET AND POTPOURRI

Stitched on blue Dublin 25 over two threads, the finished design size is 7⅞″ × 2⅜″. The fabric was cut 10″ × 8″. Begin stitching 2¾″ below top 10″ edge.

FABRIC	DESIGN SIZES
Aida 11	9″ × 2⅝″
Aida 14	7⅛″ × 2⅛″
Aida 18	5½″ × 1⅝″
Hardanger 22	4½″ × 1⅜″

ANCHOR   DMC (used for sample)

Step One: Cross-stitch (two strands)

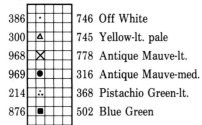

386	·	746 Off White
300	△	745 Yellow-lt. pale
968	✕	778 Antique Mauve-lt.
969	●	316 Antique Mauve-med.
214	∴	368 Pistachio Green-lt.
876	■	502 Blue Green

Stitch Count: 99 × 29

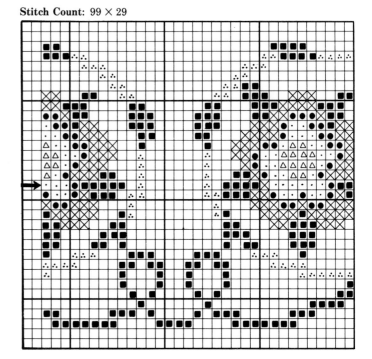

MATERIALS for pillow
Completed cross-stitch on blue Dublin 25 over two
    threads; matching thread
⅜ yards of unstitched blue Dublin 25 for pillow
½ yard of blue fabric for pocket lining and corded
    piping
2¼ yards of small cording
Stuffing

All seam allowances are ¼″.

1 Cut the stitched Dublin 8½″ × 6″ with the top of design 1″ from the top edge and centered horizontally. Cut two 15″ × 12″ pieces from the unstitched Dublin for pillow front and back. Also cut one 8½″ × 6″ piece from blue fabric for pocket lining and a 1″-wide bias strip, piecing as needed, to equal 2¼ yards. Make 2¼ yards of corded piping.

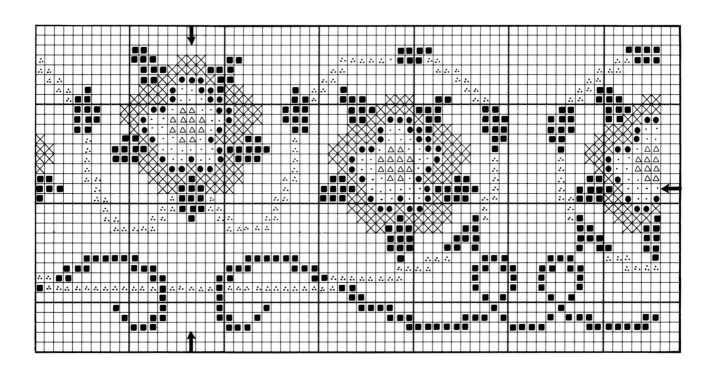

2 Stitch piping to right side of design piece, clipping corners of seam allowance. Then stitch remaining piping to right side of one 15″ × 12″ unstitched piece.

3 With right sides of design piece and lining together, stitch on stitching line for piping around design, leaving a small opening. Turn through opening and slipstitch opening closed.

4 Place pocket on right side of unstitched piece, centered horizontally and 1¼″ from bottom 15″ edge. Stitch sides and bottom edges in the gutter between design piece and piping.

5 With right sides of two 15″ × 12″ Dublin pieces together, stitch on stitching line of piping around sides leaving a small opening. Clip corners of seam allowance. Turn through opening and stuff firmly. Slipstitch the opening closed.

MATERIALS for potpourri bags
⅛ **yard each of mauve, apricot and mint green chintz; matching thread**
1¼ **yards of blue satin cording**
Potpourri

All seam allowances are ¼″.

1 Cut two pieces of fabric 8″ × 4″ from each color of chintz. Cut satin cording into three 13″ pieces.

2 With right sides together, stitch sides and bottom edges. Clip the corners. Turn. Fold over top ¼″ twice and stitch hem by hand.

3 Fill bags with potpourri. Tie a knot on each end of cording and tie around each bag.

CAT AND RABBIT

Stitched on white Quaker Cloth 28 over two threads, the finished design size is 4⅞″ × 4⅝″. The fabric was cut 11″ × 11″.

FABRIC	DESIGN SIZES
Aida 11	6¼″ × 5⅞″
Aida 14	4⅞″ × 4⅝″
Aida 18	3⅞″ × 3⅝″
Hardanger 22	3⅛″ × 3″

ANCHOR   DMC (used for sample)

Step One: Cross-stitch (two strands)

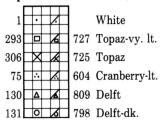

1		White
293		727 Topaz-vy. lt.
306		725 Topaz
75		604 Cranberry-lt.
130		809 Delft
131		798 Delft-dk.

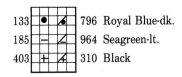

133		796 Royal Blue-dk.
185		964 Seagreen-lt.
403		310 Black

Step Two: Backstitch (one strand)

403	310 Black

Stitch Count: 69 × 65

Stitched on white Quaker Cloth 28 over two threads, the finished design size is 4⅞" × 4⅞". The fabric was cut 11" × 11".

FABRIC	DESIGN SIZES
Aida 11	6⅛" × 6⅛"
Aida 14	4⅞" × 4⅞"
Aida 18	3¾" × 3¾"
Hardanger 22	3⅛" × 3⅛"

ANCHOR   DMC (used for sample)

Step One: Cross-stitch (two strands)

1	White
323	722 Orange Spice-lt.
75	604 Cranberry-lt.
98	553 Violet-med.
130	809 Delft
131	798 Delft-dk.
229	700 Christmas Green-bright
403	310 Black

Step Two: Backstitch (one strand)

131	798 Delft-dk. (in lettering)
229	700 Christmas Green-bright (grass blades)
403	310 Black (all else)

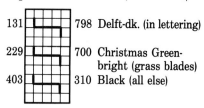

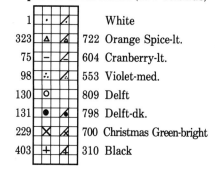

Stitch Count: 68 × 68

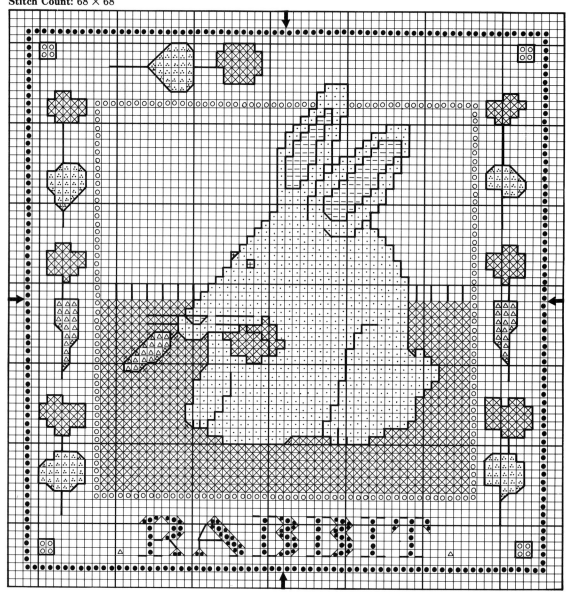

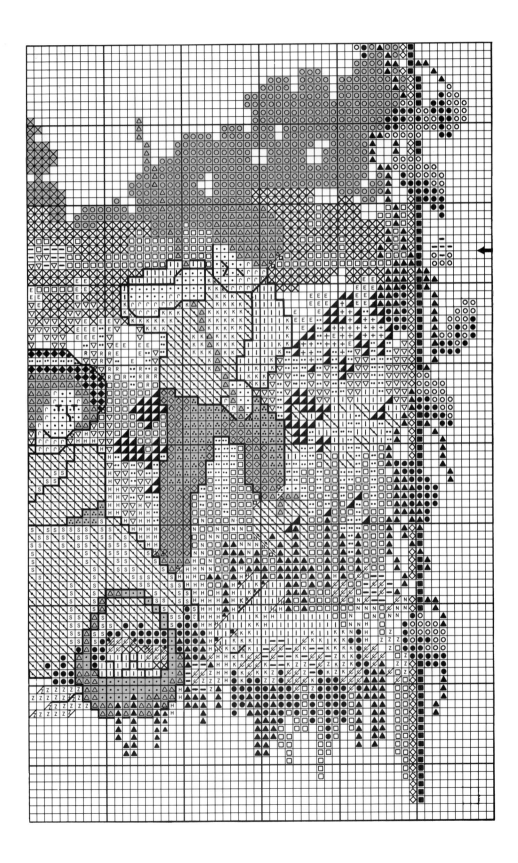

85

ONE ELEGANT GOOSE

Wing

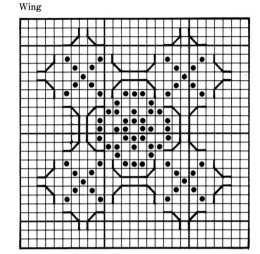

The design was stitched on pink Dublin Linen 25 over two threads. See Step 1 of instructions before stitching. The heavy black lines on the graph show the placement for the repeats.

Gusset

DMC Marlitt (used for sample)

Step One: Cross-stitch (two strands)

948	+	1213 Peach Flesh-vy. lt.
761	△	1019 Salmon-lt.
223	●	1207 Coral Pink-med.

Step Two: Backstitch (one strand)

| 223 | | 1207 Coral Pink-med. |

Body

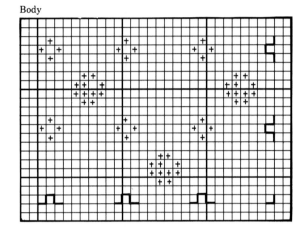

MATERIALS

⅜ yard of pink Dublin Linen (includes fabric needed for all design pieces; see Step 1); matching thread
⅜ yard of lightweight fusible interfacing
⅛ yard of pink satin for corded piping
1 yard of small cording
Stuffing
Dressmakers' pen

All seam allowances are ¼".

1 Make patterns for goose body, wing and gusset, transferring all information. Trace onto linen the number of times indicated on pattern and allow for ¼" seam allowance to be added to each piece. Stitch design #1 on body pieces, #2 on two wing pieces and #3 on gusset piece.

2 Cut all pieces from linen, adding ¼" seam allowance. Fuse interfacing to wrong side of all design pieces following manufacturer's directions. Cut 1"-wide

bias from pink satin, piecing as needed to equal 36". Make 36" of corded piping.

3 Stitch piping to wing design pieces. Pin fleece to wrong side of wing design piece. With right sides together, stitch wing design piece and unstitched wing together leaving a small opening. Turn. Repeat for second wing. Slipstitch the opening closed. Mark and stitch quilting lines on each wing.

4 Stitch darts in both body pieces. With right sides together, stitch body pieces together around head and back, backstitching at marks for gusset.

5 Place right sides of body and gusset together as indicated on pattern. Stitch one side of gusset between body seams; backstitch. Repeat on second side, leaving a small opening. Turn. Stuff firmly. Slipstitch the opening closed. Slipstitch wings to body.

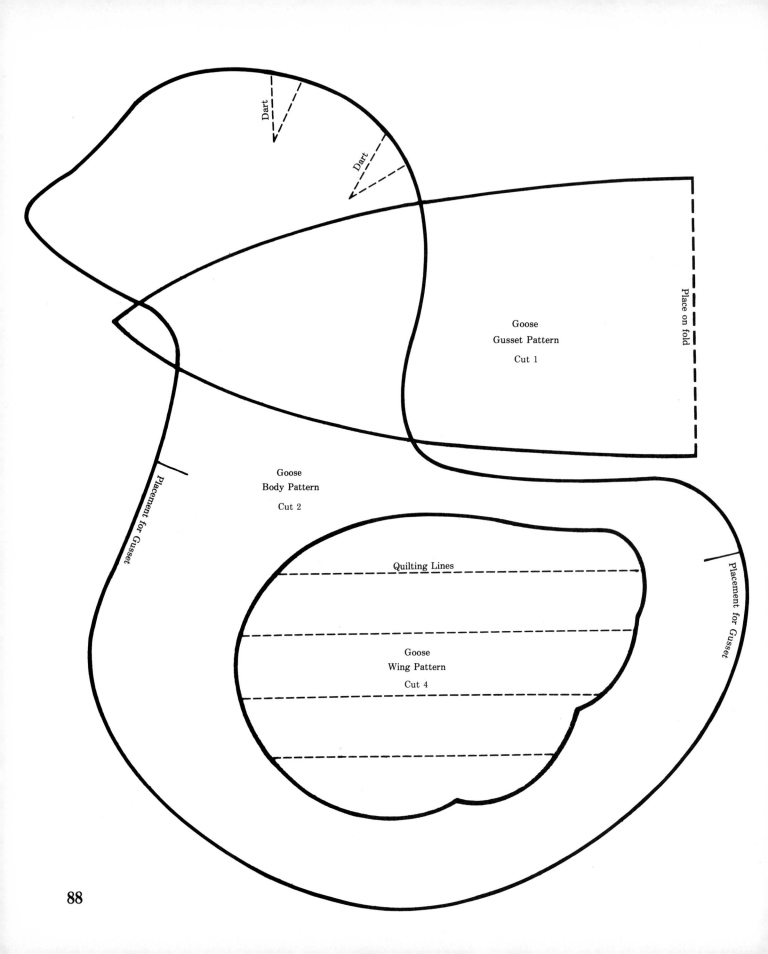

Dart

Dart

Goose
Gusset Pattern

Cut 1

Place on fold

Placement for Gusset

Goose
Body Pattern

Cut 2

Quilting Lines

Placement for Gusset

Goose
Wing Pattern

Cut 4

88

HANDKERCHIEF SACHETS

Each design was stitched with Waste Canvas 14 over one thread on a linen handkerchief; see instructions. The Waste Canvas was cut 6″ × 3″ for each.

FABRIC	DESIGN SIZES #1	DESIGN SIZES #2
Aida 11	1⅞″ × 1¼″	1⅞″ × ⅞″
Aida 14	1½″ × 1″	1½″ × ¾″
Aida 18	1⅛″ × ¾″	1⅛″ × ½″
Hardanger 22	1″ × ⅝″	1″ × ½″

FABRIC	DESIGN SIZES #3	DESIGN SIZES #4
Aida 11	⅞″ × ⅞″	3⅛″ × 1¼″
Aida 14	¾″ × ¾″	2½″ × 1″
Aida 18	½″ × ½″	2″ × ¾″
Hardanger 22	½″ × ½″	1⅝″ × ⅝″

FABRIC	DESIGN SIZES #5	DESIGN SIZES #6
Aida 11	3⅛″ × 1″	4″ × 1″
Aida 14	2½″ × ¾″	3⅛″ × ¾″
Aida 18	2″ × ⅝″	2⅜″ × ⅝″
Hardanger 22	1⅝″ × ½″	2″ × ½″

ANCHOR   DMC (used for sample)

Step One: Cross-stitch (two strands)

ANCHOR		DMC	
893	o	224	Shell Pink-lt.
968	−	778	Antique Mauve-lt.
969	✕	316	Antique Mauve-med.
869	▽	3042	Antique Violet-lt.
871	▪	3041	Antique Violet-med.
920	◇	932	Antique Blue-lt.
921	●	931	Antique Blue-med.
875	+	503	Blue Green-med.
876	▲	502	Blue Green

Step Two: Backstitch (one strand)

876		502	Blue Green

#1 Stitch Count: 21 × 14

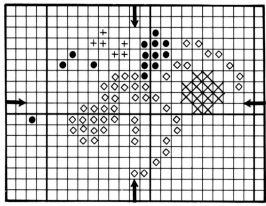

The center of design is 4¼″ from the center of the top edge.

#2 Stitch Count: 21 × 10

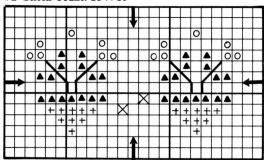

The center of design is 4½″ from the center of the top edge.

#3 Stitch Count: 9 × 9

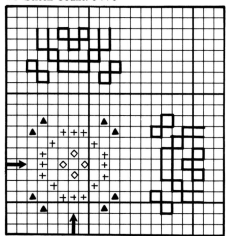

The center of design is 1″ diagonally from the corner. The heavy black lines on the graph show the placement for the repeats.

#4 Stitch Count: 35 × 14

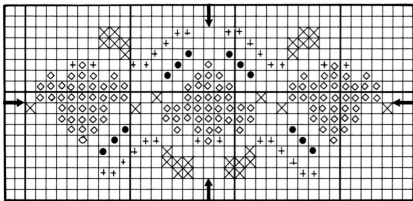

The center of design on left sachet (see photo) is 2¾″ diagonally from the corner. The center of right sachet is 4¼″ from the center of the top edge.

#5 Stitch Count: 35 × 11

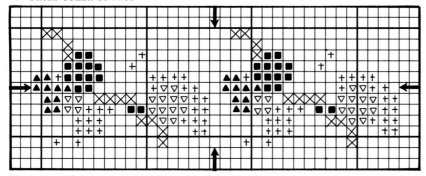

The center of design is 4¼″ from the center of the top edge.

#6 Stitch Count: 43 × 11

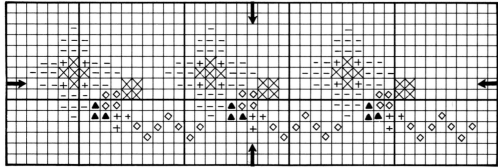

The center of design is 4¼″ from the center of the top edge.

MATERIALS for one sachet

Completed cross-stitch on men's
    18″ × 18″ linen handkerchief
2 yards of ¾″-wide white flat lace
    for finishing all edges
OR 18″ of ¾″-wide white flat lace
    for finishing a corner
One 3½″-wide Styrofoam ball
Potpourri
½ yard of ⅛″-wide pale yellow silk
    ribbon

1 Stitch white lace to all sides of handkerchief OR stitch two strips diagonally below design on one corner; see photo.

2 Hollow out part of the inside/top of the Styrofoam ball and fill with potpourri. You may wish to cut a slice off the bottom to make the sachet stable.

3 Gather handkerchief around the ball and position design; see photo. Tie with ribbon.

CRESCENT FOREST

Stitched on green Glenshee Linen 29 over two threads, the finished design size is 9⅝″ × 6¾″. The fabric was cut 16″ × 13″.

FABRIC	DESIGN SIZES
Aida 11	13⅛″ × 9⅜″
Aida 14	10¼″ × 7⅜″
Aida 18	8″ × 5¾″
Hardanger 22	6½″ × 4⅝″

ANCHOR   DMC (used for sample)

Step One: Cross-stitch (two strands)

926			Ecru
292	+		3078 Golden Yellow-vy. lt.
293	=		727 Topaz-vy. lt.
347	◇		402 Mahogany-vy. lt.
324	U		922 Copper-lt.
892			225 Shell Pink-vy. lt.
24	P		776 Pink-med.
66	+		3688 Mauve-med.
69	△		3687 Mauve
70			3685 Mauve-dk.
869			3042 Antique Violet-lt. (one strand)
007	W		Pink Balger (one strand)

101	○		327 Antique Violet-dk.
158	▽		747 Sky Blue-vy. lt.
159	□		827 Blue-vy. lt.
159			827 Blue-vy. lt.(one strand)
	B		Sky Blue Balger (one strand)
128			800 Delft-pale
167	○		519 Sky Blue
160	□		813 Blue-lt.
160			813 Blue-lt. (one strand)
014	N		Sky Blue Balger (one strand)
147	✕		312 Navy Blue-lt.
264	∵		772 Pine Green-lt.
214	G		966 Baby Green-med.
216	■		367 Pistachio Green-dk.
879	✕		890 Pistachio Green-ultra dk.
362	▼		437 Tan-lt.
392	∷		642 Beige Gray-dk.
898			611 Drab Brown-dk.
371	◆		433 Brown-med.
400	●		414 Steel Gray-dk.

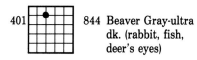

Step Two: Backstitch (one strand)

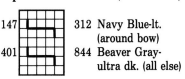

147		312 Navy Blue-lt. (around bow)
401		844 Beaver Gray-ultra dk. (all else)

Step Three: French Knots (one strand)

401	●	844 Beaver Gray-ultra dk. (rabbit, fish, deer's eyes)

Stitch Count: 144 × 103

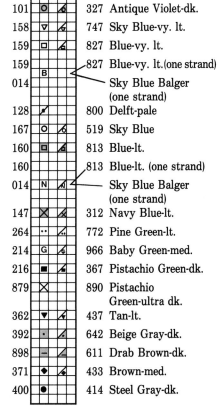
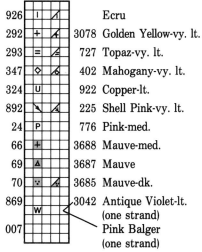
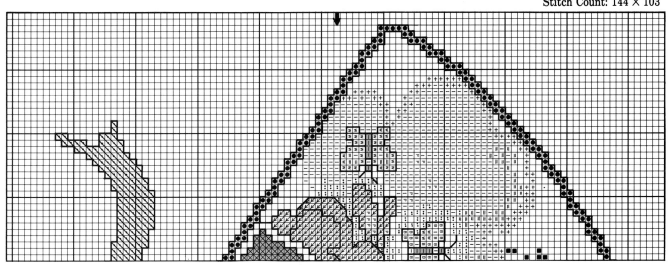

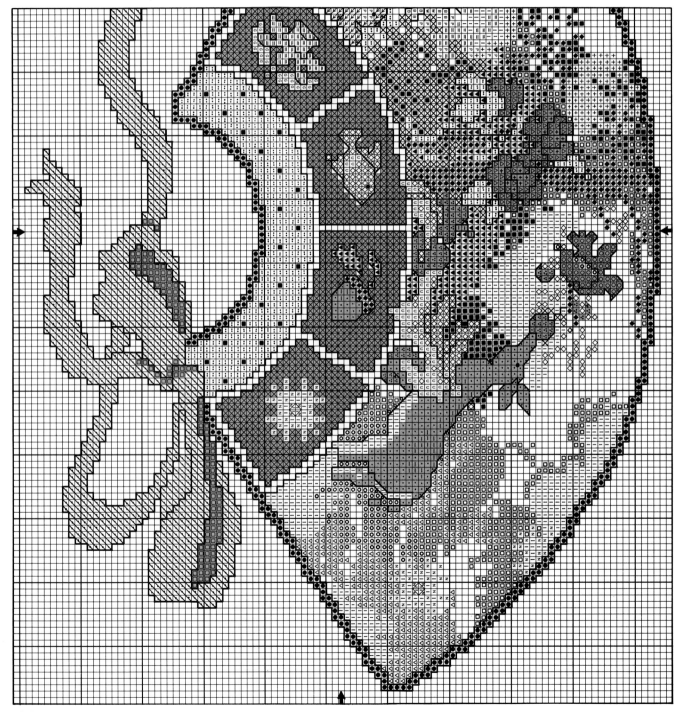

94

SCRAPBOOK MEMORIES

Stitched on white Jobelan 28 over two threads, the finished design size is 5¾ × 7⅝". The fabric was cut 12" × 14".

FABRIC	DESIGN SIZES
Aida 11	7¾" × 9¾"
Aida 14	5¾" × 7⅝"
Aida 18	4½" × 6"
Hardanger 22	3⅝" × 4⅞"

ANCHOR   DMC (used for sample)

Step One: Cross-stitch (two strands)

292	O	3078	Golden Yellow-vy. lt.
887	M	3046	Yellow Beige-med.
10	W	352	Coral-lt.
11	G	3328	Salmon-med.
24	+	776	Pink-med.
27	◇	899	Rose-med.
42	╱	309	Rose-deep
160	−	813	Blue-lt.
145	□	334	Baby Blue-med.
147	◆	312	Navy Blue-lt.
920	↗	932	Antique Blue-lt.
921	●	931	Antique Blue-med.
213	·	369	Pistachio Green-vy. lt.
246	▲	319	Pistachio Green-vy. dk.
266	∴	471	Avocado Green-vy. lt.
243	X	988	Forest Green-med.
900	↗	3024	Brown Gray-vy. lt.
392	U	642	Beige Gray-vy. lt.
380	E	839	Beige Brwon-dk.
399	△	318	Steel Gray-lt.
401	■	413	Pewter Gray-dk.

Step Two: Backstitch (one strand)

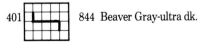

401		844	Beaver Gray-ultra dk.

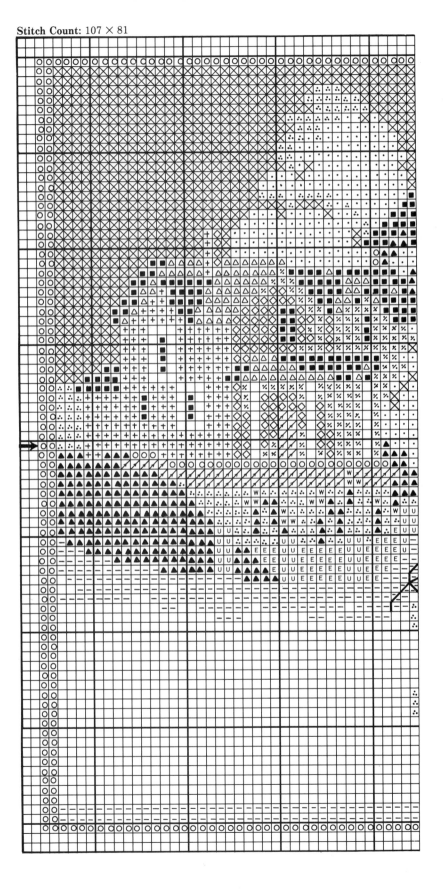

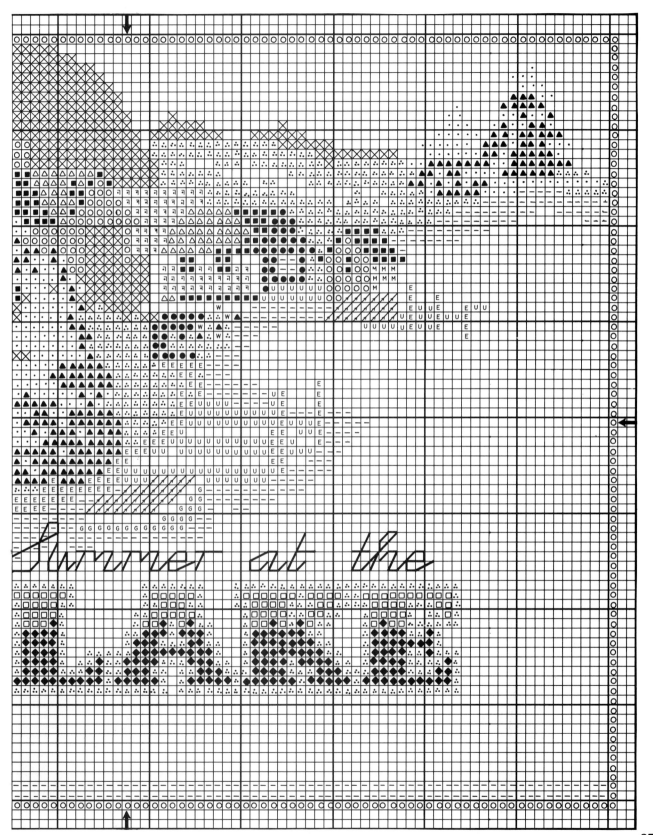

Stitched on white Jobelan 28 over two threads, the finished design size is 5¾ × 7¾". The fabric was cut 12" × 14".

FABRIC	DESIGN SIZES
Aida 11	7¼" × 9⅞"
Aida 14	5¾" × 7¾"
Aida 18	4½" × 6"
Hardanger 22	3⅝" × 4⅞"

ANCHOR   DMC (used for sample)

Step One: Cross-stitch (two strands)

891	676	Old Gold-lt.
366	951	Sportsman Flesh-vy. lt.
4146	950	Sportsman Flesh-lt.
914	3064	Sportsman Flesh-med.
893	224	Shell Pink-lt.
894	223	Shell Pink-med.
158	775	Baby Blue-lt.
120	794	Cornflower Blue-lt.
121	793	Cornflower Blue-med.
167	598	Turquoise-lt.
168	597	Turquoise
264	472	Avocado Green-ultra lt.
267	470	Avocado Green-lt.
388	3033	Mocha Brown-vy. lt.
379	840	Beige Brown-med.
397	762	Pearl Gray-vy. lt.
399	318	Steel Gray-lt.
401	844	Beaver Gray-ultra dk.

Step Two: Backstitch (one strand)

401	844	Beaver Gray-ultra dk.

Step Three: French knots (one strand)

401	844	Beaver Gray-ultra dk.

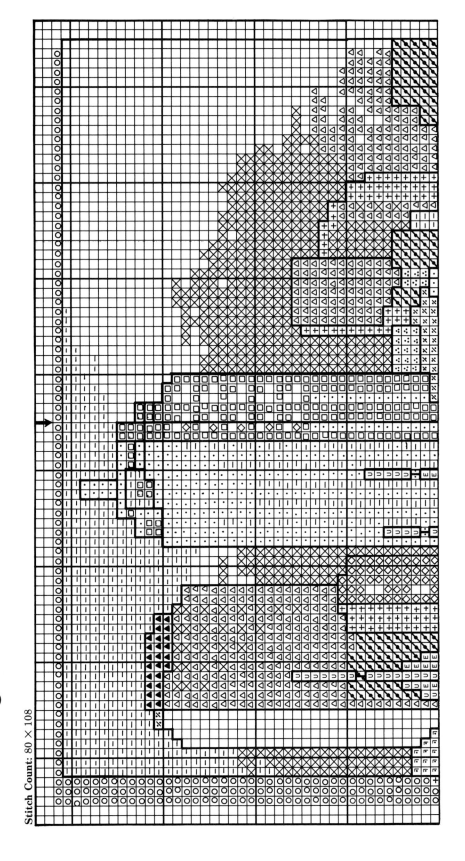

Stitch Count: 80 × 108

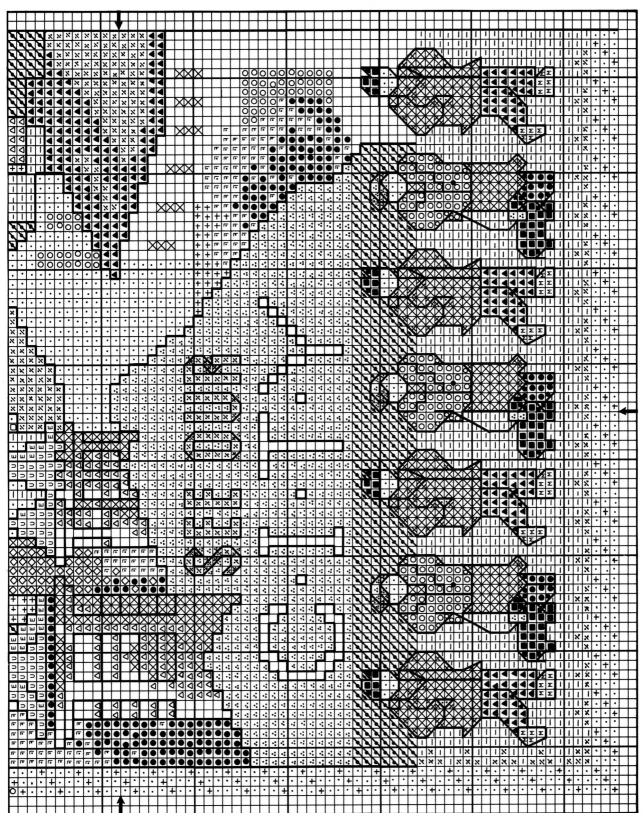

Stitched on white Jobelan 28 over two threads, the finished design size is 5⅞″ × 7⅞″. The fabric was cut 12″ × 14″.

Stitch Count: 110 × 82

FABRIC	DESIGN SIZES
Aida 11	7½″ × 10″
Aida 14	5⅞″ × 7⅞″
Aida 18	4½″ × 6⅛″
Hardanger 22	3¾″ × 5″

ANCHOR   DMC (used for sample)

Step One: Cross-stitch (two strands)

300	745 Yellow-lt. pale
316	970 Pumpkin-lt.
48	818 Baby Pink
49	963 Dusty Rose-vy. lt.
26	957 Geranium-pale
66	3688 Mauve-med.
105	209 Lavender-dk.
99	552 Violet-dk.
158	828 Blue-ultra vy. lt.
159	3325 Baby Blue
160	813 Blue-lt.
161	826 Blue-med.
203	954 Nile Green
204	912 Emerald Green-lt.
205	911 Emerald Green-med.
933	543 Beige Brown-ultra vy. lt.
362	437 Tan-lt.
349	301 Mahogany-med.
376	842 Beige Brown-vy. lt.
378	841 Beige Brown-lt.
379	840 Beige Brown-med.

Step Two: Backstitch (one strand)

203	954 Nile Green (green letters)
204	912 Emerald Green-lt. (border)
905	645 Beaver Gray-vy. dk. (all else)

Step Three: French knot (one strand)

905	645 Beaver Gray-vy. dk.

Stitched on white Jobelan 28 over two threads, the finished design size is 5¾ × 7⅞″. The fabric was cut 12″ × 14″.

Stitch Count: 110 × 81

FABRIC	DESIGN SIZES
Aida 11	7⅜″ × 10″
Aida 14	5¾″ × 7⅞″
Aida 18	4½″ × 6½″
Hardanger 22	3⅝″ × 5″

ANCHOR   DMC (used for sample)

Step One: Cross-stitch (two strands)

300	745 Yellow-lt. pale
366	951 Sportsman Flesh-vy. lt.
4146	950 Sportsman Flesh-lt.
914	3064 Sportsman Flesh-med.
8	761 Salmon-lt.
49	3689 Mauve-lt.
49	3689 Mauve-lt. (one strand)
	Pink Balger (one strand)
69	3687 Mauve
104	210 Lavender-med.
869	3042 Antique Violet-lt.
871	3041 Antique Violet-med.
101	327 Antique Violet-dk.
158	747 Sky Blue-vy. lt.
120	794 Cornflower Blue-lt.
920	932 Antique Blue-lt.
940	792 Cornflower Blue-dk.
203	954 Nile Green
215	368 Pistachio Green-lt.
216	320 Pistachio Green-med.
376	842 Beige Brown-vy. lt.
379	840 Beige Brown-med.
398	415 Pearl Gray
401	413 Pewter Gray-dk.

Step Two: Backstitch

69	3687 Mauve (sign)
376	842 Beige Brown-vy. lt. (trees)
401	413 Pewter Gray-dk. (all else)

Step Three: French knot (one strand)

401	413 Pewter Gray-dk.

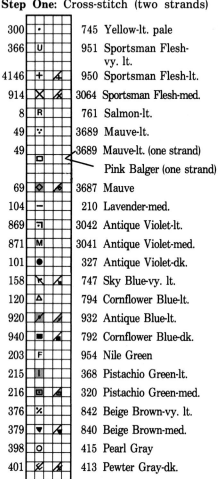

102

AUTUMN

RARE MOMENT

Stitched on Linaida 14 over one thread, the finished design size is 18⅝″ × 19¼″. The fabric was cut 32″ × 33″.

FABRIC	DESIGN SIZES
Aida 11	23⅜″ × 24½″
Aida 14	18⅝″ × 19¼″
Aida 18	14⅜″ × 15″
Hardanger 22	11⅞″ × 12¼″

ANCHOR DMC (used for sample)

Step One: Cross-stitch (two strands)

926	Ecru
891	676 Old Gold-lt.
914	3064 Sportsman Flesh-med.
5975	356 Terra Cotta-med.
5968	355 Terra Cotta-dk.
885	739 Tan-ultra vy. lt.
942	738 Tan-vy. lt.
388	3033 Mocha Brown-vy. lt.

903	3032 Mocha Brown-med.
378	841 Beige Brown-lt.
307	977 Golden Brown-lt.
308	976 Golden Brown-med.
363	436 Tan
370	434 Brown-lt.
914	3064 Sportsman Flesh-med. (one strand)
349	301 Mahogany-med. (one strand)
349	301 Mahogany-med.
351	400 Mahogany-dk.
352	300 Mahogany-vy. dk.
357	801 Coffee Brown-dk.
381	938 Coffee Brown-ultra dk.

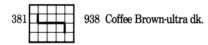

Step Two: Backstitch (one strand)

381	938 Coffee Brown-ultra dk.

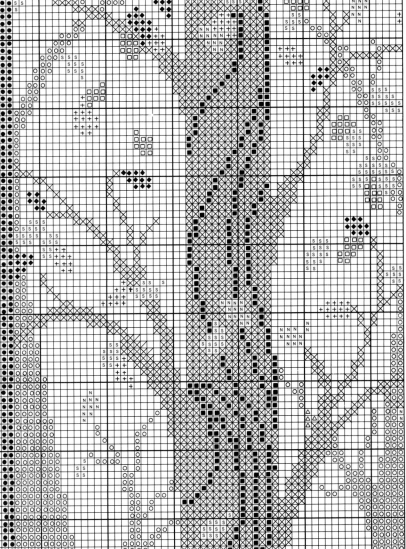

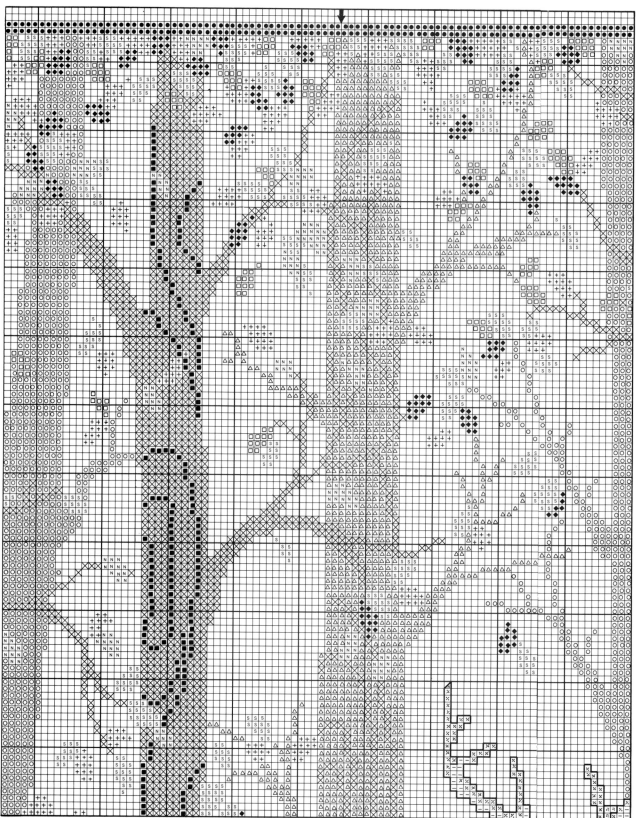

108

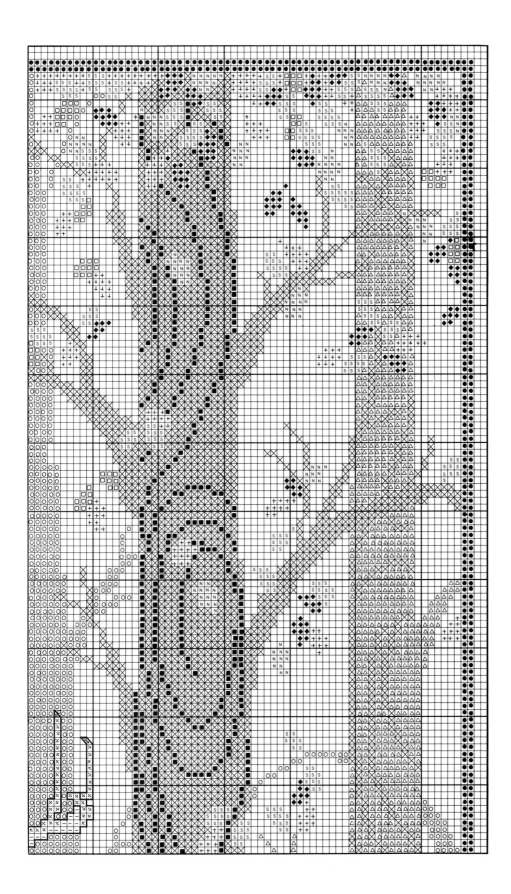

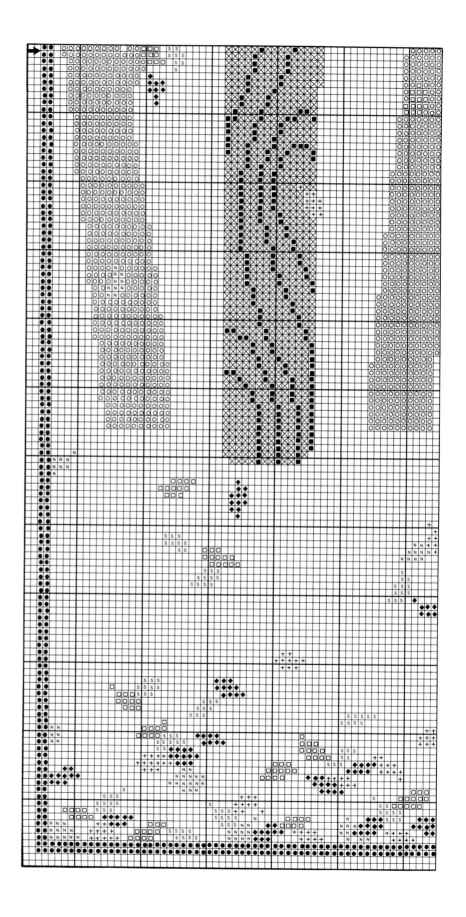

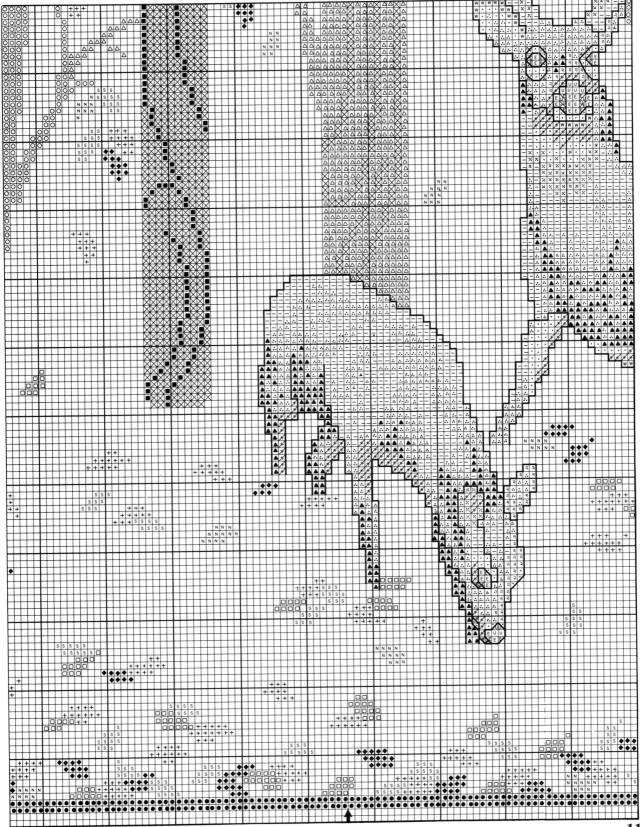

111

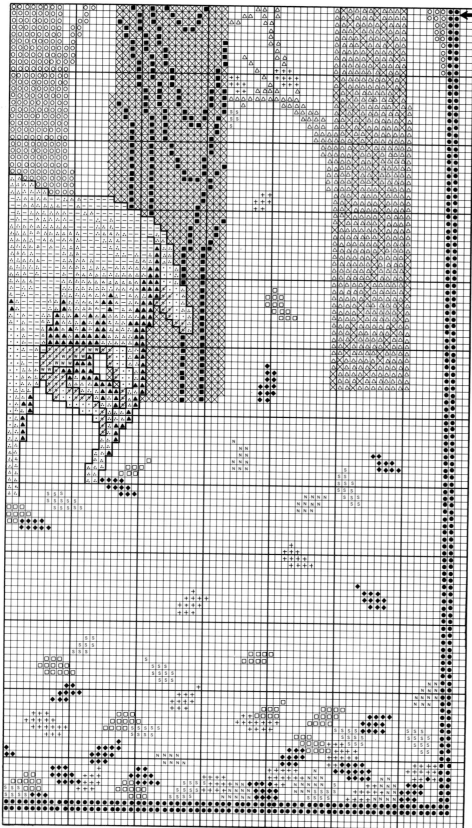

112

The border for "A Rare Moment" was stitched on Linaida 14 over one thread. Begin stitching three threads away from the dark brown border on side or bottom edge; see diagram. Continue stitching border around entire center design.

ANCHOR DMC (used for sample)

Step One: Cross-stitch (two strands)

ANCHOR		DMC	
308	☐	976	Golden Brown-med.
363	∴	436	Tan
370	▲	434	Brown-lt.

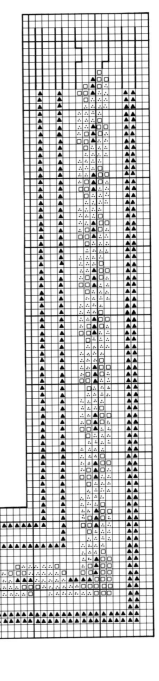

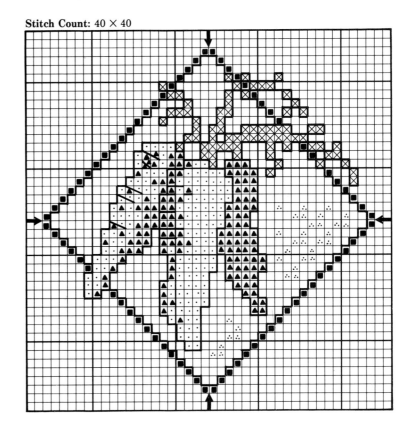

THE KITCHEN PANTRY

Stitched on white Belfast Linen 32 over two threads, the finished design size is 2½″ × 2½″. The fabric was cut 11″ × 11″.

Vegetables on Silk (framed)

Stitched on silk canvas 30 over one thread, the finished design size is 1⅜″ × 1⅜″. The fabric was cut 4″ × 4″.

FABRIC	DESIGN SIZES
Aida 11	3⅝″ × 3⅝″
Aida 14	2⅞″ × 2⅞″
Aida 18	2¼″ × 2¼″
Hardanger 22	1⅞″ × 1⅞″

ANCHOR   DMC (used for sample)

Step One: Cross-stitch (two strands)

886	▫		677 Old Gold-vy. lt.
891	■		676 Old Gold-lt.
8	·		353 Peach Flesh
10	▲		352 Coral-lt.
27	−	◿	899 Rose-med.
42	○	◢	309 Rose-deep
167	∴		519 Sky Blue
214	▲	◿	368 Pistachio Green-lt.
216	⊠	◿	367 Pistachio Green-dk.

Step Two: Backstitch (one strand)

149	⌐		336 Navy Blue

Stitch Count: 40 × 40

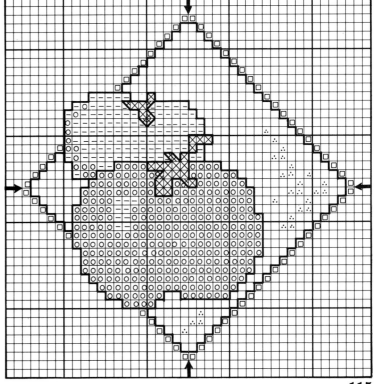

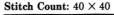

115

Stitch Count: 40 × 40

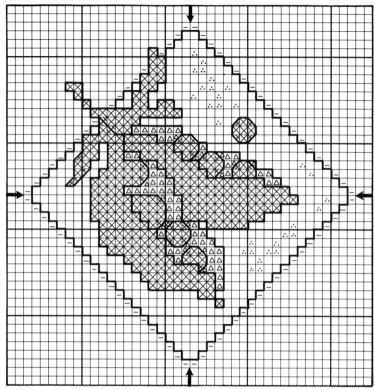

MATERIALS
Completed cross-stitch on white Belfast Linen 32; matching thread

1 Stitch with a narrow zigzag stitch 1″ from all edges.

2 Fray all edges to edge of zigzag stitch.

" C H A S E   N A T U R E   A W A Y ,
A N D   I T   R E T U R N S   A T   A
G A L L O P "

— P. N. Destouches —

116

THE SCARECROW

Stitched on cream Perforated
Paper 15 over one , the finished
design size for the arms is
2⅞″ × 1⅜″; the legs are
1⅛″ × 3⅜″; the body is 2″ × 4¼″.
Use one 9″ × 12″ sheet of paper.

FABRIC	DESIGN SIZES	DESIGN SIZES
	Arms	Legs
Aida 11	3¾″ × 1⅞″	1⅜″ × 4⅜″
Aida 14	2⅞″ × 1⅜″	1⅛″ × 3⅜″
Aida 18	2¼″ × 1⅛″	⅞″ × 2⅝″
Hardanger 22	1⅞″ × ⅞″	⅝″ × 2⅛″

FABRIC	DESIGN SIZES
	Body
Aida 11	2½″ × 5⅜″
Aida 14	2″ × 4¼″
Aida 18	1½″ × 3¼″
Hardanger 22	1¼″ × 2⅝″

ANCHOR   DMC (used for sample)

Step One: Cross-stitch (two strands)

306	●	725	Topaz
4146	·	754	Peach Flesh-lt.
8	+	353	Peach Flesh
323	−	722	Orange Spice-lt.
326	O	720	Orange Spice-dk.
969	△	316	Antique Mauve-med.
970	■	315	Antique Mauve-dk.
42	E	3350	Dusty Rose-vy. dk.
145	□	334	Baby Blue-med.
147	✕	312	Navy Blue-lt.
168	∴	807	Peacock Blue
246	▲	986	Forest Green-vy. dk.
380	B	839	Beige Brown-dk.

Step Two: Backstitch (one strand)

246		986	Forest Green-vy. dk. (stems)
147		312	Navy Blue-lt. (all else)

Stitch Count: 28 × 59 (body)

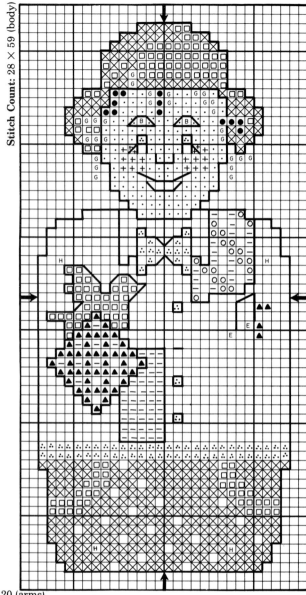

Stitch Count: 41 × 20 (arms)

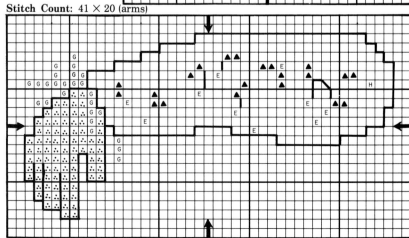

Step Three: Ribbonwork (see instructions)

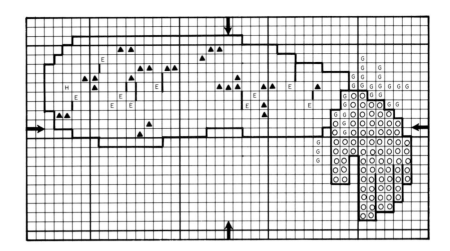

	G		
1/8"-wide bright yellow silk ribbon

Option: Floss

308 | G | 782 Topaz-med.

Step Four: Buttons (see instructions)

H		
(connect arms and legs)

MATERIALS

Completed cross-stitch on cream Perforated Paper 15
1/8"-wide bright yellow silk ribbon
Two 1/4"-wide red buttons
Two 1/4"-wide dark blue buttons

1 If using ribbon for "G" symbol, thread through area and tie knots on front of design to secure.

2 Carefully cut one hole outside the design area, rounding out curves in some areas.

3 Match the "H" symbol on the arms to the shoulder of the sleeve with the arms behind. Attach buttons with ribbon through both layers of paper and tie a knot in back. Repeat to attach the legs.

Stitch Count: 15 × 48 (legs)

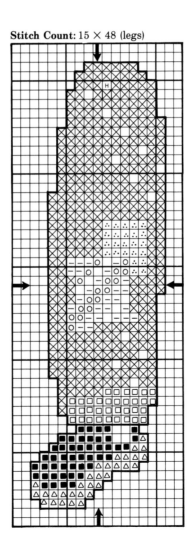

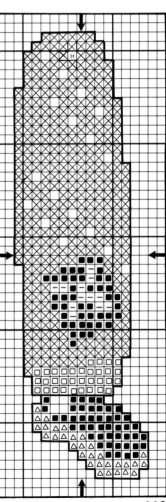

119

Stitched on raw Belfast Linen 32 over two threads, the finished design size for one motif is 2⅝″ × 1½″. The fabric was cut 18″ × 15″.

Mark the placement for the design center 4″ from the top 15″ edge. Stitch a motif on each side of center mark. The heavy black lines on the graph show the placement for the repeats.

FABRIC	DESIGN SIZES
Aida 11	3⅞″ × 2⅛″
Aida 14	3″ × 1¾″
Aida 18	2⅜″ × 1⅜″
Hardanger 22	1⅞″ × 1⅛″

ANCHOR   DMC (used for sample)

Step One: Cross-stitch (two strands)

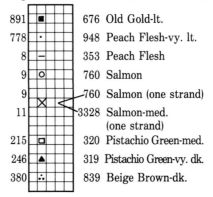

891	676	Old Gold-lt.
778	948	Peach Flesh-vy. lt.
8	353	Peach Flesh
9	760	Salmon
9	760	Salmon (one strand)
11	3328	Salmon-med. (one strand)
215	320	Pistachio Green-med.
246	319	Pistachio Green-vy. dk.
380	839	Beige Brown-dk.

Step Two: Backstitch (one strand)

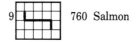

9	760	Salmon

Stitch Count: 42 × 24 (for one motif)

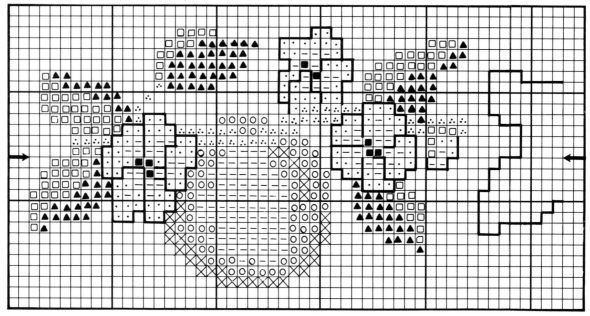

Stitched on raw Belfast Linen 32 over two threads, the finished design size for one motif is 3¼″ × 1¼″. The fabric was cut 18″ × 15″.

Mark the placement for the design center 4″ from the top 15″ edge. Stitch a motif on each side of center mark. The heavy black lines on the graph show the placement for the repeats.

FABRIC	DESIGN SIZES
Aida 11	4¾″ × 1¾″
Aida 14	3¾″ × 1⅜″
Aida 18	2⅞″ × 1″
Hardanger 22	2⅜″ × ⅞″

ANCHOR   DMC (used for sample)

Step One: Cross-stitch (two strands)

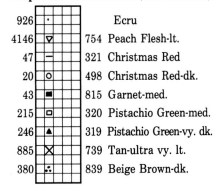

926		Ecru
4146	▽	754 Peach Flesh-lt.
47	−	321 Christmas Red
20	○	498 Christmas Red-dk.
43	■	815 Garnet-med.
215	□	320 Pistachio Green-med.
246	▲	319 Pistachio Green-vy. dk.
885	✕	739 Tan-ultra vy. lt.
380	∴	839 Beige Brown-dk.

Step Two: Backstitch (one strand)

9		760 Salmon

Stitch Count: 52 × 19 (for one motif)

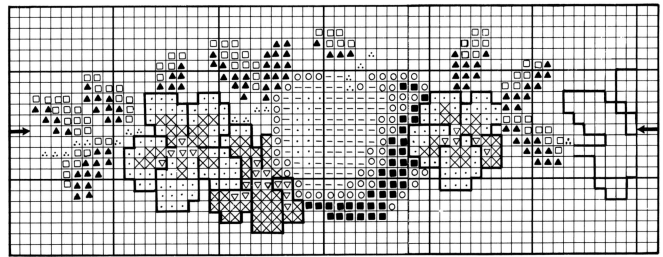

MATERIALS

Completed cross-stitch on raw Belfast Linen 32; matching thread

One 2¼″ × 15″ piece of raw Belfast Linen 32 for handle

½ yard of dark green or purple or red satin for lining and corded piping; matching thread

1¾ yards small cording

All seam allowances are ¼″.

1 Enlarge and make pattern. Place pattern on design piece with top edge 1″ above design and centered horizontally. Cut one basket piece from linen and one from satin for lining. Cut one 2½″ × 15″ piece from satin to line handle. Also cut 1¼″-wide bias, piecing as needed, to equal 63″. Make 63″ of corded piping.

2 Cut piping into two 15″, two 9″ and two 5″ pieces. Stitch to edges of linen handle piece and to matching outside edges of design piece.

3 Stitch lining to handle piece with right sides together, stitching on stitching line of piping. Turn.

4 Place design piece right side up on flat surface. With linen side down, place handle over design piece, centering handle ends on 5″ ends of design piece. Place lining over design piece with right sides together and matching corners. Stitch all edges, leaving a small opening. Clip corners. Turn. Slipstitch the opening closed.

5 Fold two sides of basket together. Slipstitch carefully. Repeat with remaining corners.

1 square = 1″

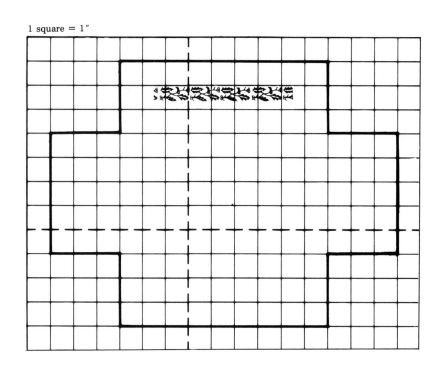

HARVEST HARE

Stitched on cream Aida 14 over one thread, the finished design size is 11⅜″ × 11″. The fabric was cut 18″ × 17″.

FABRIC	DESIGN SIZES
Aida 11	14½″ × 14″
Aida 18	8⅞″ × 8½″
Hardanger 22	7¼″ × 7″

ANCHOR DMC (used for sample)

Step One: Cross-stitch (two strands)

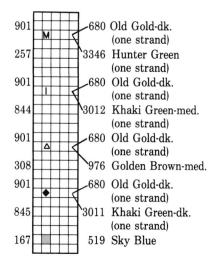

926	—	Ecru
926		Ecru (one strand)
882	S	407 Sportsman Flesh-dk. (one strand)
969	•	316 Antique Mauve-med.
891	⁄	676 Old Gold-lt.
901	N	680 Old Gold-dk.
901	●	680 Old Gold-dk. (one strand)
266		3347 Yellow Green-med. (one strand)

901	M	680 Old Gold-dk. (one strand)
257		3346 Hunter Green (one strand)
901	I	680 Old Gold-dk. (one strand)
844		3012 Khaki Green-med. (one strand)
901	△	680 Old Gold-dk. (one strand)
308		976 Golden Brown-med.
901	◆	680 Old Gold-dk. (one strand)
845		3011 Khaki Green-dk. (one strand)
167		519 Sky Blue

Stitch Count: 159 × 154

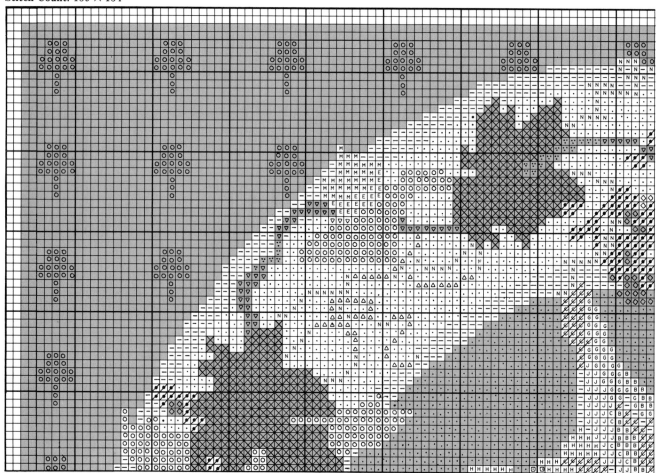

126

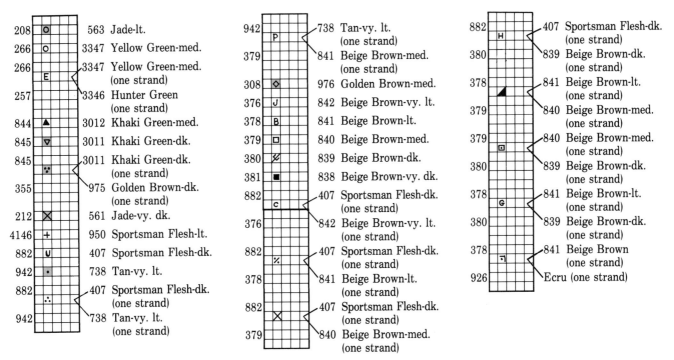

208 ○ 563 Jade-lt.

266 ○ 3347 Yellow Green-med.

266 E 3347 Yellow Green-med. (one strand)
257 ⌐ 3346 Hunter Green (one strand)

844 ▲ 3012 Khaki Green-med.

845 ▽ 3011 Khaki Green-dk.

845 ⁛ 3011 Khaki Green-dk. (one strand)
355 ⌐ 975 Golden Brown-dk. (one strand)

212 ✕ 561 Jade-vy. dk.

4146 + 950 Sportsman Flesh-lt.

882 U 407 Sportsman Flesh-dk.

942 · 738 Tan-vy. lt.

882 ∴ 407 Sportsman Flesh-dk. (one strand)
942 ⌐ 738 Tan-vy. lt. (one strand)

942 P 738 Tan-vy. lt. (one strand)
379 ⌐ 841 Beige Brown-med. (one strand)

308 ◇ 976 Golden Brown-med.

376 J 842 Beige Brown-vy. lt.

378 B 841 Beige Brown-lt.

379 ▢ 840 Beige Brown-med.

380 ⊠ 839 Beige Brown-dk.

381 ■ 838 Beige Brown-vy. dk.

882 C 407 Sportsman Flesh-dk. (one strand)
376 ⌐ 842 Beige Brown-vy. lt. (one strand)

882 ⊠ 407 Sportsman Flesh-dk. (one strand)
378 ⌐ 841 Beige Brown-lt. (one strand)

882 ✕ 407 Sportsman Flesh-dk. (one strand)
379 ⌐ 840 Beige Brown-med. (one strand)

882 H 407 Sportsman Flesh-dk. (one strand)
380 ⌐ 839 Beige Brown-dk. (one strand)

378 ◣ 841 Beige Brown-lt. (one strand)
379 ⌐ 840 Beige Brown-med. (one strand)

379 ▢ 840 Beige Brown-med. (one strand)
380 ⌐ 839 Beige Brown-dk. (one strand)

378 G 841 Beige Brown-lt. (one strand)
380 ⌐ 839 Beige Brown-dk. (one strand)

378 ⌐ 841 Beige Brown (one strand)
926 ⌐ Ecru (one strand)

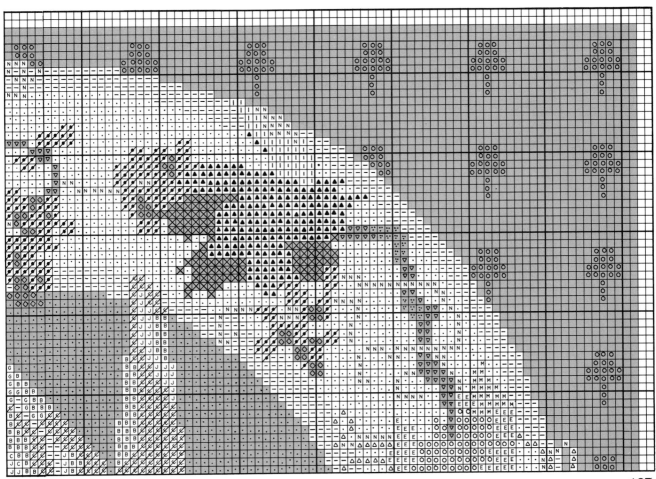

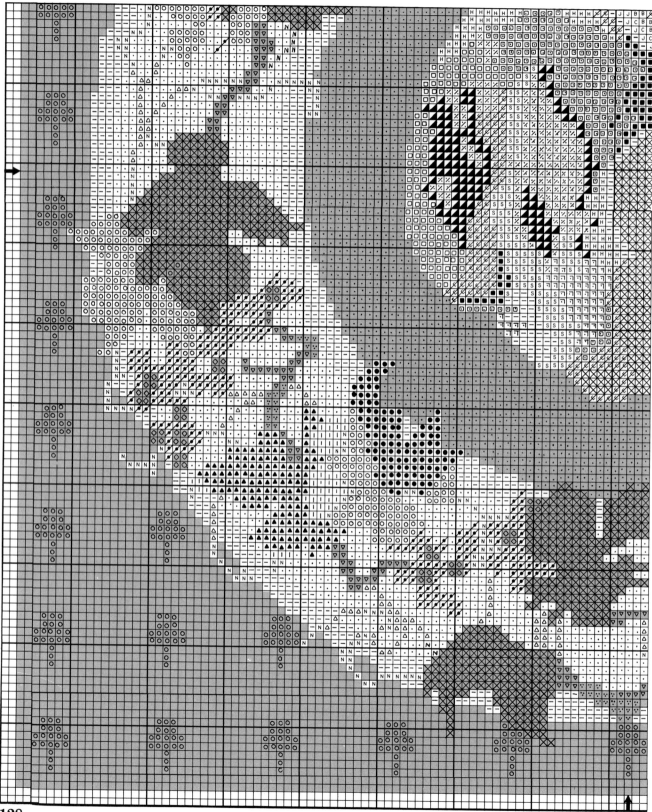

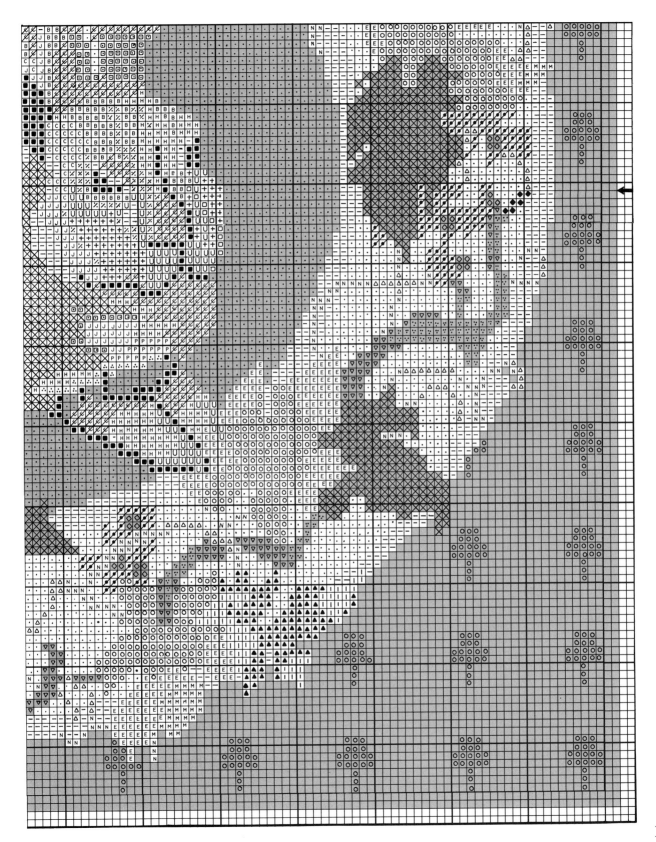

129

FOUR FORMAL HAND TOWELS

Stitched on four different colors of Lugana 25 (mushroom, moss green, pewter, and ash rose) over two threads, the finished design size for each is 10⅛″ × 1″. The fabric was cut 15″ × 27″. The center of design is 2″ from the bottom 15″ edge.

FABRIC	DESIGN SIZES
Aida 11	11½″ × 1⅛″
Aida 14	9″ × ⅞″
Aida 18	7″ × ¾″
Hardanger 22	5¾″ × ⅝″

ANCHOR   DMC (used for sample)

Step One: Cross-stitch (two strands)

894	–	223 Shell Pink-med.
970	⠔	315 Antique Mauve-dk.
921	▲	931 Antique Blue-med.
878	✕	501 Blue Green-dk.
379	○	840 Beige Brown-med.

Step Two: Backstitch (one strand)

| 401 | | 844 Beaver Gray-ultra dk. |

MATERIALS for mushroom towel

Completed cross-stitch on Lugana 25
1¼ yards of ⅛″-wide gray silk ribbon
½ yard of ¼″-wide flat gold trim

MATERIALS for moss green towel

Completed cross-stitch on Lugana 25
1¼ yards of ⅛″-wide moss green silk ribbon
½ yard of ½″-wide moss green double-sided silk trim

MATERIALS for pewter towel

Completed cross-stitch on Lugana 25
1¼ yards of ⅛″-wide light blue silk ribbon
½ yard of ½″-wide antique blue flat silk trim

MATERIALS for ash rose towel

Completed cross-stitch on Lugana 25
½ yard of lavender silk ribbon
1 yard of ½″-wide lavender silk trim

All seam allowances are ¼″.

1 Place trim in rows parallel to the design; see photo.

2 Fold ¼″ double to wrong side of the towel on all edges; stitch the hem.

Stitch Count: 126 × 13

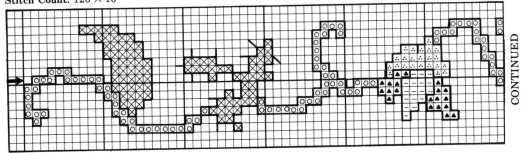

CONTINUED

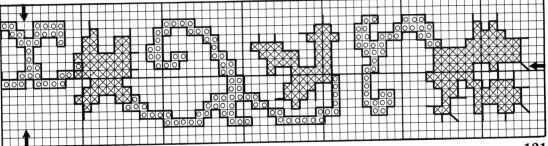

INDIAN SUMMER TABLECLOTH

The tablecloth was stitched on cream Bondeno. See diagram for cutting fabric and placement of designs. The heavy black line on the outside of the graph indicates the edge of the woven block.

FABRIC	DESIGN SIZES	DESIGN SIZES
	Acorn	Fall Leaf
Aida 11	2⅝″ × 2⅝″	2¾″ × 2¾″
Aida 14	2⅛″ × 2⅛″	2⅛″ × 2⅛″
Aida 18	1⅝″ × 1⅝″	1⅝″ × 1⅝″
Hardanger 22	1⅜″ × 1⅜″	1⅜″ × 1⅜″

FABRIC	DESIGN SIZES
	Squash
Aida 11	2¾″ × 2¾″
Aida 14	2⅛″ × 2⅛″
Aida 18	1⅝″ × 1⅝″
Hardanger 22	1⅜″ × 1⅜″

ANCHOR   DMC (used for sample)

Step One: Cross-stitch (six strands)

ANCHOR		DMC	
306	·	725	Topaz
890	X	729	Old Gold-med.
324	∴	922	Copper-lt.
349	△ ◿	921	Copper
341	●	919	Red Copper
842	−	3013	Khaki Green-lt.
844	▢	3012	Khaki Green-med.
845	▲	3011	Khaki Green-dk.
8581	+	3023	Brown Gray-lt.
378	○	841	Beige Brown-lt.
379	■	840	Beige Brown-med.

Step Two: Backstitch (two strands)

ANCHOR		DMC	
844		3012	Khaki Green-med. (loose vines on squash)
380		839	Beige Brown-dk. (all else)

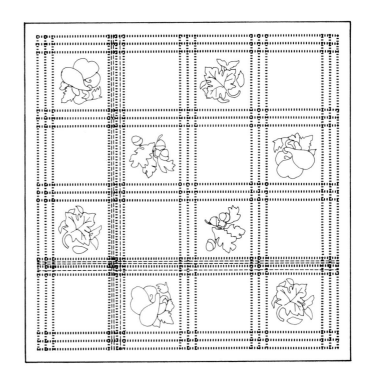

Stitch Count: 29 × 29 (acorn)

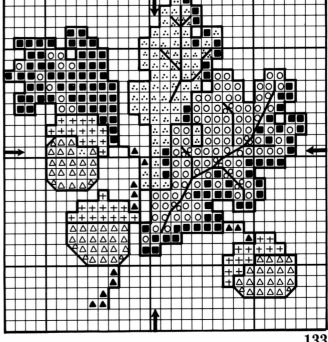

Stitch Count: 30 × 30 (fall leaf)

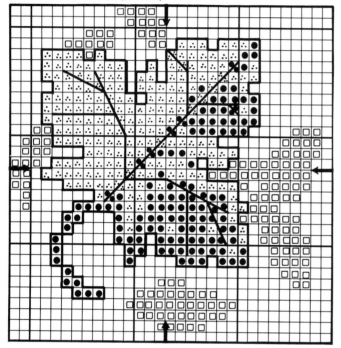

MATERIALS
Completed cross-stitch on cream Bondeno; matching
    thread
2 yards of ⅛″-wide rust silk ribbon
2 yards of ⅛″-wide golden yellow silk ribbon
2 yards of ⅛″-wide moss green silk ribbon
Large-eyed needle

1 Thread ribbon into large-eyed needle and sew a running stitch between two vertical woven bands; see diagram for placement. Each stitch is over nine threads and under three threads. Working left to right and top to bottom, begin with rust ribbon, then yellow and green.

2 Fold under ¾″ double to sides and stitch the hem by hand, mitering the corners. (The process is simpler by hand than by machine.)

Stitch Count: 30 × 30 (squash)

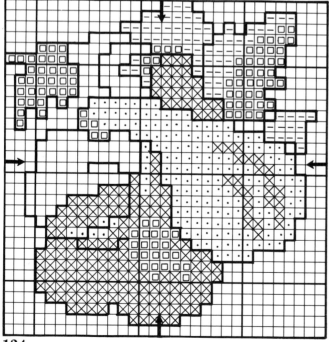

134

SOUTHWESTERN BORDER

Stitched on sand Dublin Linen 25 over one thread, the finished design size for one motif is 1⅝″ × 1⅛″. The fabric was cut 5″ by the distance around the basket plus 2″. Repeat the design to fill the distance. The heavy black lines on the graph show the placement for the repeats.

FABRIC	DESIGN SIZES
Aida 11	3⅝″ × 2½″
Aida 14	2⅞″ × 2″
Aida 18	2¼″ × 1½″
Hardanger 22	1⅞″ × 1¼″

ANCHOR   DMC (used for sample)

Step One: Cross-stitch (one strand)

ANCHOR		DMC	
869	–	3042	Antique Violet-lt.
168	o	597	Turquoise
922	▲	930	Antique Blue-dk.
849	▫	927	Slate Green-med.
876	∴	502	Blue Green
362	✕	437	Tan-lt.

Stitch Count: 40 × 28 (for one motif)

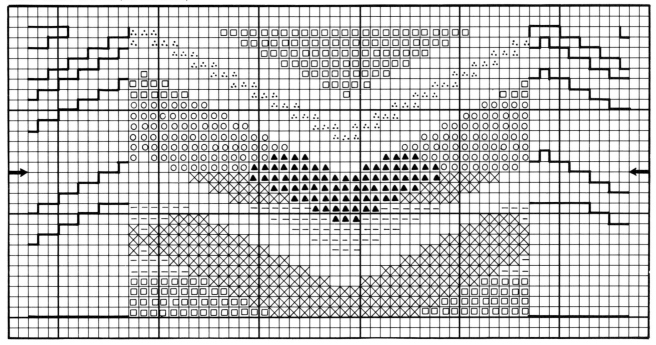

MATERIALS
Completed cross-stitch on sand Dublin Linen 25; matching thread

All seam allowances are ¼″.

1 Measure distance around basket. Cut design piece 4″ wide with the design centered and the length of the distance around the basket with ½″ on each end.

2 Fold the design piece with right sides together to measure 2″ wide. Stitch the length of the piece. Turn. Refold with the design centered and the seam at the center back.

3 Place on basket. Mark where ends meet to fit basket. Remove. Fold under ½″ inside of first end. Then slide other end inside the first. Slipstitch securely. Place band on basket. Tack as needed.

POPCORN POUCHES

Stitched on cream Aida 14 over one thread, the finished design size is 2⅜″ × 3½″. The fabric was cut 7″ × 10″.

FABRIC	DESIGN SIZES
Aida 11	3⅛″ × 4½″
Aida 18	1⅞″ × 2¾″
Hardanger 22	1½″ × 2¼″

ANCHOR   DMC (used for sample)

Step One: Cross-stitch (two strands)

886		677	Old Gold-vy. lt.
295		726	Topaz-lt.
306		725	Topaz
326		720	Orange Spice-dk.
159		3325	Baby Blue
266		3347	Yellow Green-med.
268		3345	Hunter Green-dk.
942		738	Tan-vy. lt.
363		436	Tan
381		938	Coffee Brown-ultra dk.

Step Two: Backstitch (one strand)

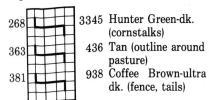

268		3345	Hunter Green-dk. (cornstalks)
363		436	Tan (outline around pasture)
381		938	Coffee Brown-ultra dk. (fence, tails)

Stitch Count: 34 × 49

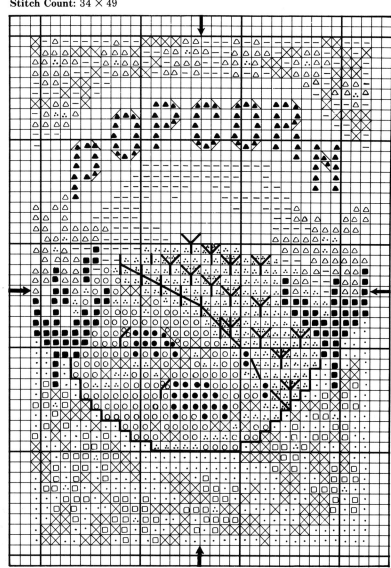

VICTORIAN BOUQUET

Stitched on ivory Damask 14 over one thread, the finished design size for is 4¼″ × 5⅝″. The fabric was cut 9″ × 10″. Also needed are twenty-two pearl beads and ten small assorted buttons.

FABRIC	DESIGN SIZES
Aida 11	5½″ × 7⅛″
Aida 14	4¼″ × 5⅝″
Aida 18	3⅜″ × 4⅜″
Hardanger 22	2¾″ × 3⅝″

ANCHOR   DMC (used for sample)

Step One: Cross-stitch (two strands)

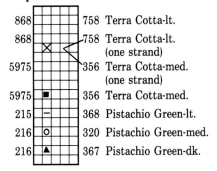

868		758 Terra Cotta-lt.
868		758 Terra Cotta-lt. (one strand)
5975	✕	356 Terra Cotta-med. (one strand)
5975	■	356 Terra Cotta-med.
215	−	368 Pistachio Green-lt.
216	○	320 Pistachio Green-med.
216	▲	367 Pistachio Green-dk.

Step Two: Buttons and Beads

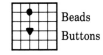

● Beads
▼ Buttons

Stitch Count: 60 × 79

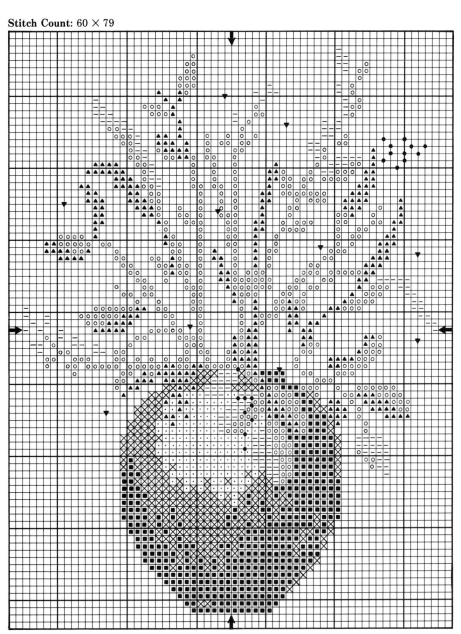

WINTER

the angel of the
Lord
came upon them
and the glory of the
Lord
shone round about
them

The sweetest flower that grows
I give you as we part.
For you it is a rose
For me it is my heart.

THE SWEETEST FLOWER

Stitched on ash rose Aida 14 over one thread, the finished design size is 4⅝″ × 3″. The fabric was cut 11″ × 9″. See suppliers for beads.

FABRIC	DESIGN SIZES
Aida 11	5¾″ × 3⅞″
Aida 14	4⅝″ × 3″
Aida 18	3½″ × 2⅜″
Hardanger 22	2⅞″ × 1⅞″

ANCHOR   DMC (used for sample)

Step One: Cross-stitch (two strands)

72 ▲ 902 Garnet-vy. dk.

Step Two: Backstitch (two strands)

72 902 Garnet-vy. dk. (lettering)

Step Three: Beads

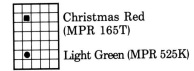

■ Christmas Red (MPR 165T)

● Light Green (MPR 525K)

MATERIALS
Completed cross-stitch on pink Aida 14; matching thread
One 5″ × 7″ piece fabric for back
One 5″ × 7″ piece of fusible web
½ yard of 2″–wide flat pink lace
½ yard of ⅜″–wide pink brocade ribbon
½ yard of ⅜″–wide light green satin ribbon
1⅝ yard of ⅙″–wide light green satin ribbon
1⅝ yard of ⅙″–wide burgundy satin ribbon
One small burgundy button
One 1″–wide heart-shaped pearl button
Seven red beads
Seven light green beads
Water-based varnish
Sponge brush applicator
Glitter spray
Waxed paper
Glue

Stitch Count: 64 × 42

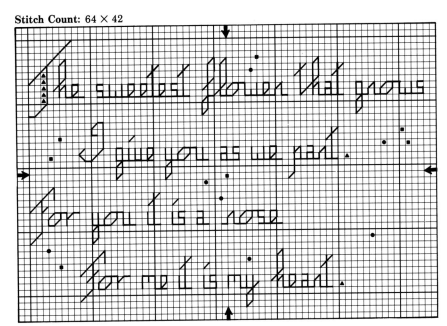

1 Select floral pattern from print fabric. Trim around design carefully and fuse to Aida (see photo for placement) following manufacturer's directions.

2 Complete Step 1 of Varnishing in General Instructions.

3 Make pattern for oval that is 4½″ × 6½″. Center over design and cut out. Stitch pink lace to edge, beginning and ending at lower right of design and easing somewhat so lace will lie flat.

4 Complete Steps 2 through 5 of Varnishing in General Instructions.

5 Thread ⅛″-wide ribbon through pink lace, beginning and ending at lower right of design. Trim ends as desired.

6 Handling ⅜″-wide brocade and satin ribbons as one, fold into bow. Secure to lower right of design by stitching through button, ribbons and design piece.

7 Sew burgundy button to upper left of design on pink lace. Glue beads to design piece.

PRETTY 'N' PINK

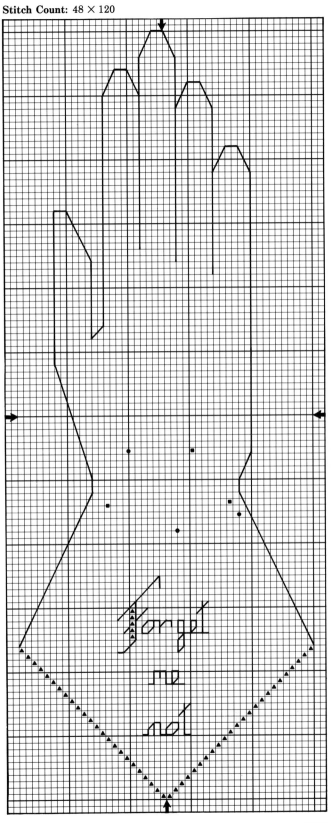

Stitched on ash rose Aida 14 over one thread, the finished design size for the glove is 3⅜″ × 8⅝″, the fan is 6½″ × 3⅞″. The fabric was cut 12″ × 14½″ for the glove and 13″ × 10″ for the fan. See suppliers for beads.

FABRIC	DESIGN SIZES Glove	DESIGN SIZES Fan
Aida 11	4⅜″ X 10⅞″	8¼″ X 5″
Aida 18	2⅝″ X 6⅝″	5″ X 3″
Hardanger 22	2⅛″ X 5½″	4⅛″ X 2½″

ANCHOR **DMC (used for sample)**

Step One: Cross-stitch (two strands)

ANCHOR	Symbol	DMC
894	○	223 Shell Pink-med.
72	▲	902 Garnet-vy. dk.
922	✕	930 Antique Blue-dk.

Step Two: Backstitch (two strands)

ANCHOR	DMC
894	223 Shell Pink-med. (date and initials on fan)
72	902 Garnet-vy. dk. (lettering and outline on glove)
922	930 Antique Blue-dk. (lettering on fan)

Step Three: Beads

Symbol	Bead
■	Christmas Red (MPR 165T)
●	Light Green (MPR 525K)

Stitch Count: 48 × 120

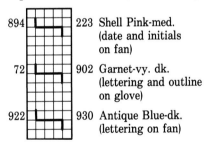

Stitch Count: 91 × 55

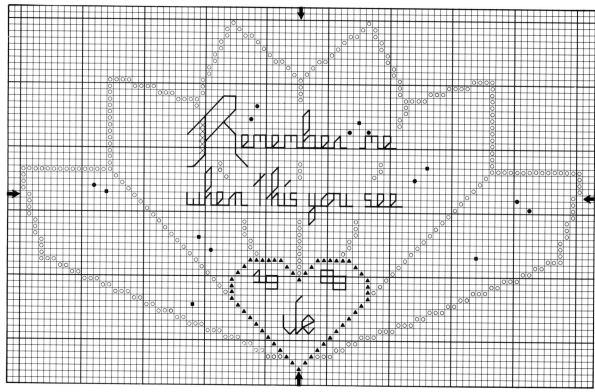

MATERIALS for glove
Completed cross-stitch on pink Aida 14
One small piece of floral print fabric for design
One 4″ × 9″ piece of fabric for back
One piece of fusible web (4″ × 9″ plus enough for floral print)
Five small, decorative buttons
One small heart locket
Three red beads
Three light green beads

MATERIALS for fan
Completed cross-stitch on pink Aida 14
Three small pieces of floral print fabric for design
One 4½″ × 7″ piece of fabric for back
One piece of fusible web (4½″ × 7″ plus enough for floral prints)
Two small decorative buttons
Six red beads
Nine light green beads

MATERIALS for both
One 36″ piece of each color of floss: DMC 224, 223, 221, 3041, 932, 931
Two 6″ pieces of one color of floss
1 yard metallic gold thread
Water-based varnish

162

Sponge brush applicator
Glitter spray
Waxed paper
Glue

1 Select floral pattern from print fabric. Trim around design carefully and fuse to Aida (see photo for placement) following manufacturer's directions.

2 Complete Steps 1-5 of Varnishing in General Instructions. (Do not cut between thumb and finger on glove.)

3 Attach buttons using floss in either matching or contrasting colors. Glue beads at random.

4 To make the tassel, cut one 36″ piece of each color of floss used in design. Also cut two 6″ pieces of one color. Handling the gold metallic thread with the 36″ pieces of floss, wrap all around two fingers. Thread a 6″ length through the loops; knot securely. Wrap the second 5″ piece tightly around the top of the loops near knot; secure. Cut the fold in the loops opposite the knot. Trim tassel to desired length. Thread one end of first 6″ piece into needle and sew through design piece.

Good Tidings

Stitched on white Perforated Paper 15 over one, the finished design size is 2⅝" × 2⅛". The paper was cut 9" × 9".

FABRIC	DESIGN SIZES
Aida 11	3½" × 2⅞"
Aida 14	2¾" × 2¼"
Aida 18	2⅛" × 1¾"
Hardanger 22	1¾" × 1⅜"

ANCHOR   DMC (used for sample)

Step One: Cross-stitch (two strands)

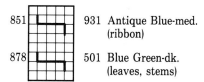

886	677 Old Gold-vy. lt.
893	224 Shell Pink-lt.
969	316 Antique Mauve-med.
970	315 Antique Mauve-dk.
850	932 Antique Blue-lt.
851	931 Antique Blue-med.
900	928 Slate Green-lt.
876	502 Blue Green

Step Two: Backstitch (one strand)

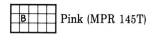

| 851 | 931 Antique Blue-med. (ribbon) |
| 878 | 501 Blue Green-dk. (leaves, stems) |

Step Three: Beads

B Pink (MPR 145T)

Stitch Count: 39 × 31

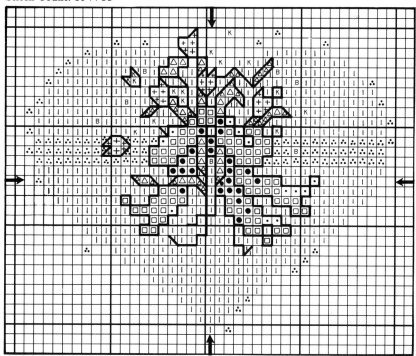

MATERIALS for flower design

Completed cross-stitch on white perforated paper
One 7″ × 8″ piece of rose mat board
½ yard of ⅜″–wide dark green grosgrain ribbon
Double-sided tape
Glue
Black pen for message

1 Cut perforated paper 4″ × 4½″ with design centered. Mark placement for design on mat board; see diagram.

2 Write message on mat board and add vertical lines to right edge. Tape the design to mat board. Place ribbon over design; see diagram. Glue ends to back.

MATERIALS for small heart design

Completed cross-stitch on white perforated paper
One 4″ × 5″ piece of green mat board
5″ of ⅛″–wide burgundy satin ribbon
Double-sided tape
Glue
Dark green pen for message

1 Cut perforated paper 2″ × 2½″ with design centered. Mark placement for design on board; see diagram.

2 Write message and decorate mat board. Tape the design to mat board; see diagram. Place ribbon ½″ above bottom edge of card. Glue ends to back.

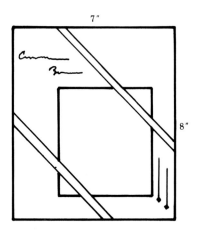

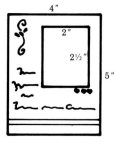

Stit
thro
The

FA
Aid
Aid
Aid
Ha

AN

Ste

38
414
91
5
15
16
16
16
90
84
77
87
87
93
88
94
30
30
93
3
3
3
3
3
4

St

9
3

# TWO FESTIVE BUNNIES

Stitched on ivory Linda 27 over two threads, the finished design size is 1⅞" × 3¾". The fabric was cut 9" × 9".

FABRIC	DESIGN SIZES
Aida 11	2⅜" × 4⅝"
Aida 14	1⅞" × 3⅝"
Aida 18	1½" × 2⅞"
Hardanger 22	1⅛" × 2⅜"

ANCHOR   DMC (used for sample)

Step One: Cross-stitch (two strands)

1	−	White
886	·	3047 Yellow Beige-lt.
891	△	676 Old Gold-lt.
6	■	353 Peach Flesh
8	+	761 Salmon-lt.
76	∷	603 Cranberry
13	○	349 Coral-dk.
19	✕	817 Coral Red-vy. dk.
95	▫	554 Violet-lt.
98	●	553 Violet-med.
238	▲	703 Chartreuse
403	z	310 Black

Step Two: Backstitch (one strand)

373		3045 Yellow Beige-dk. (rabbit)
403		310 Black (packages)

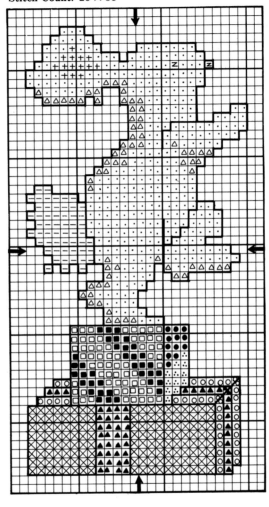

1 square = 1"

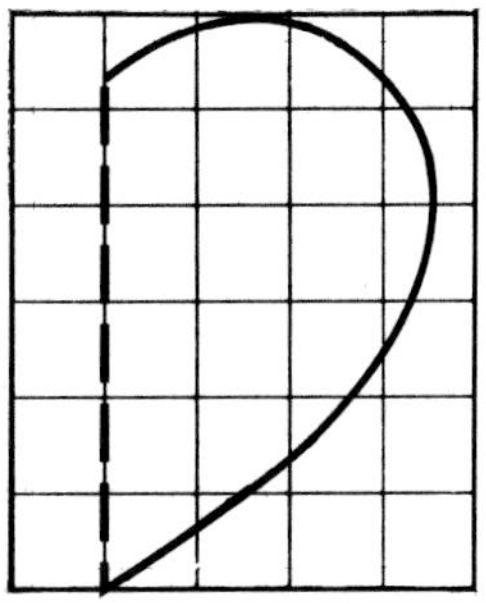

MATERIALS for heart pillow
Completed cross-stitch on ivory Linda 27; matching thread
One 8" × 8" square of ivory Linda 27 or matching fabric for back
¼ yard of striped fabric for gusset
Stuffing

All seam allowances are ¼".

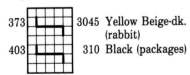 Enlarge and make pattern. Center the pattern over the design and cut one heart. Also cut one heart from the 8" × 8" square of fabric for the back.

2 Cut 1¼"-wide strips from striped fabric, piecing as needed, to equal 40" for gusset. Stitch gathering threads in both long edges. Gather to measure 20" dispersing fullness evenly.

3 Stitch the right sides of gusset and design piece together, beginning and ending at center bottom. Join ends of the gusset.

4 Pin back to gusset. Stitch, leaving a small opening. Clip the curved seam allowance. Turn. Stuff moderately. Slipstitch the opening closed. Remove gathering threads.

Stitched on ivory Linda 27 over two threads, the finished design size is 3⅜″ × 3⅛″. The fabric was cut 8″ × 8″.

FABRIC	DESIGN SIZES
Aida 11	4⅛″ × 4″
Aida 14	3¼″ × 3⅛″
Aida 18	2½″ × 2⅜″
Hardanger 22	2⅛″ × 2″

ANCHOR   DMC (used for sample)

Step One: Cross-stitch (two strands)

1	–		White
886	·		3047 Yellow Beige-lt.
373	●		3045 Yellow Beige-dk.
891	△		676 Old Gold-lt.
881	+		945 Sportsman Flesh
868	○		758 Terra Cotta-lt.
20	▫		498 Christmas Red-dk.
72	∴		902 Garnet-vy. dk.
266	✕		3347 Yellow Green-med.
246	▲		895 Christmas Green-dk.
403	z		310 Black

Step Two: Backstitch (one strand)

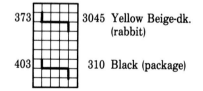

373		3045 Yellow Beige-dk. (rabbit)
403		310 Black (package)

MATERIALS for square pillow
Completed cross-stitch on ivory Linda 27; matching thread
One 6″ × 6″ square of ivory Linda 27 or matching fabric for back
¼ yard of striped fabric for gusset
Stuffing

Stitch Count: 46 × 43

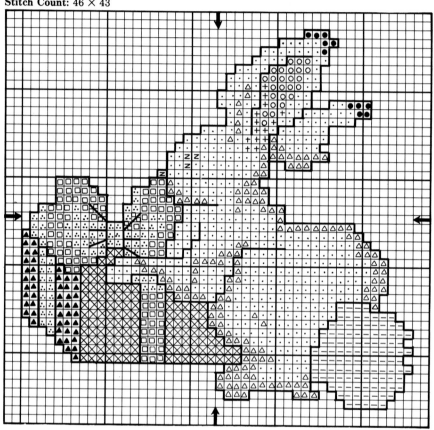

1 Trim the design piece to 6″ × 6″ with the design centered.

2 Follow Steps 2, 3 and 4 of heart pillow directions.

SHIMMERING SNOWFLAKES

Stitched on white Belfast Linen 32 over two threads, the finished design size for one motif of #1 is 4¼″ × 1¾″; #2 is 4½″ × 2″; #3 is 5″ × 2″. The heavy black lines on the graph show the placement for the repeats.

Snowflake tree skirt:

Repeat design to make eight 20″ strips from the three different designs. See suppliers for beads.

Snowflake stocking:

Repeat design to make one 9 ½″ strip for cuff and one 18″ strip. See suppliers for beads.

FABRIC	DESIGN SIZES #1	DESIGN SIZES #2
Aida 11	6¼″ X 2 ½″	6½″ X 2⅞″
Aida 14	4⅞″ X 2″	5⅛″ X 2¼″
Aida 18	3⅞″ X 1 ½″	4″ X 1¾″
Hardanger 22	3⅛″ X 1 ¼″	3¼″ X 1⅜″

FABRIC	DESIGN SIZES #3
Aida 11	7¼″ X 2⅞″
Aida 14	5¾″ X 2¼″
Aida 18	4½″ X 1¾″
Hardanger 22	3⅝″ X 1⅜″

ANCHOR/DMC (used for cover sample)

Step One: Cross-stitch (two strands)

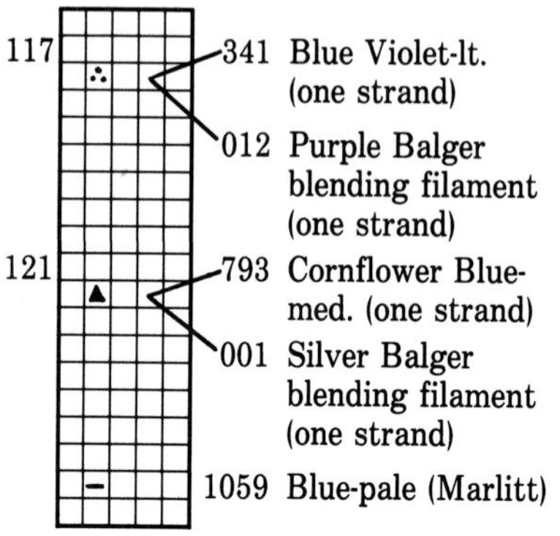
117
341 Blue Violet-lt. (one strand)
012 Purple Balger blending filament (one strand)
121
793 Cornflower Blue-med. (one strand)
001 Silver Balger blending filament (one strand)
1059 Blue-pale (Marlitt)

#1 **Stitch Count:** 69 × 28

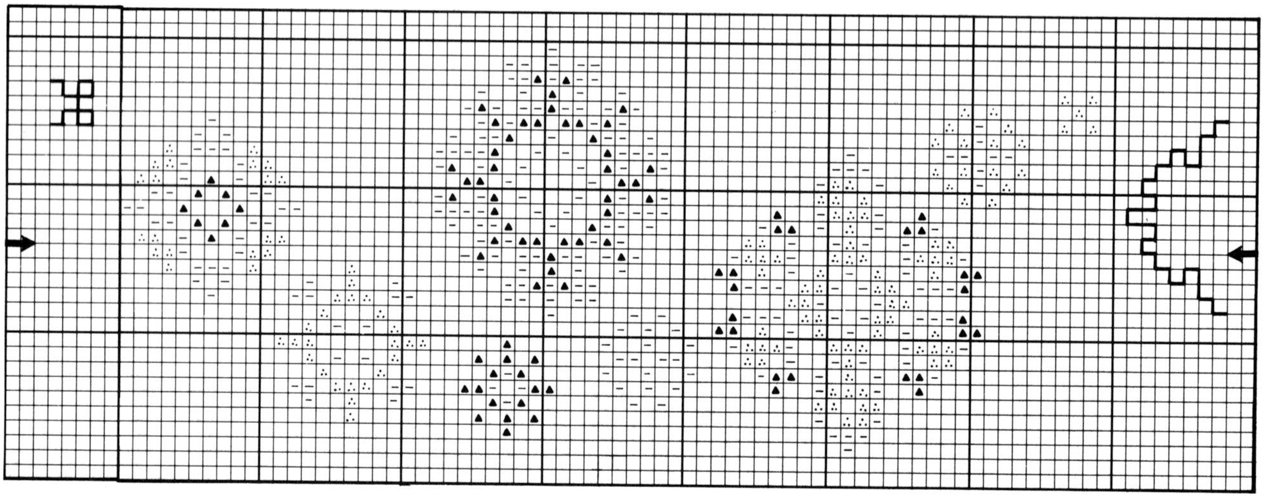

#2 **Stitch Count:** 71×31

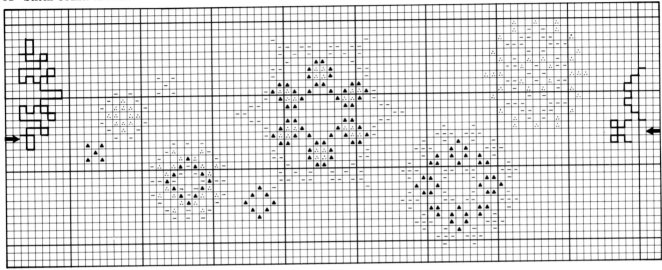

#3 **Stitch Count:** 80×31

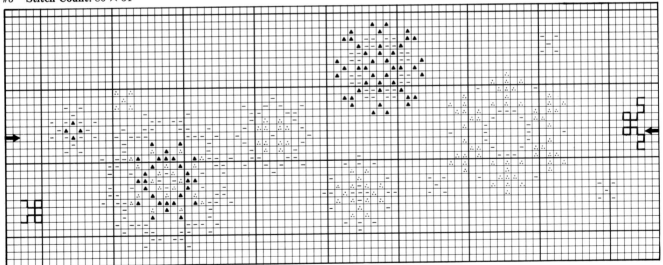

MATERIALS for tree skirt

Completed cross-stitch on white Belfast Linen 32;
   matching thread
3 yards of linen-like white fabric
3 yards of white fabric for lining
1¾ yards of ⅛″-wide silver metallic ribbon (#1)*
3½ yards of ⅜″-wide white flat trim (#2)*
6 yards of ¼″-wide white flat trim (#3)*
2¾ yards of ⅜″-wide white flat trim (#4)*
9¼ yards of silver picot trim (#5)*
2 yards of two different ¼″-wide white flat trims (#6
   and #7)*
2 yards of ⅛″-wide white flat trim (#8)*
3 yards of ½″-wide white satin ribbon
Tracing paper for pattern
Dressmakers' pen

All seam allowances are ¼″.

1   Cut each design strip 4″ × 19″ with the design centered. Fold 1″ to the wrong side along both long edges; press.

2   Enlarge and trace the pattern for the tree skirt panel. Cut eight panels from the linen-like fabric and eight panels from the white fabric for lining.

3   Cut trims and place on panel; see diagram. Mark placement with dressmakers' pen and stitch in place, attaching design strip and silver picot trim last. Trim all ends to match the edges of the panel.

4   Place the tree skirt panels side by side, alternating the designs. Stitch the panels with right sides together leaving one seam unstitched for the center back opening. Stitch together the panels for the lining. Place the right sides of the tree skirt and lining together, matching the seams. Stitch one edge of the back opening, around the outside edge of the skirt, and the second edge of the back opening, pivoting carefully at each seam. Clip curved seam allowances; turn.

5   Slipstitch the "neck" opening closed.

6   Cut ½″-wide satin ribbon into six 18″ pieces. Mark three equal intervals on each edge of center back opening. Attach one end of one ribbon length to each mark. Tie ribbons into bows when skirt is on tree.

* See diagram for placement.

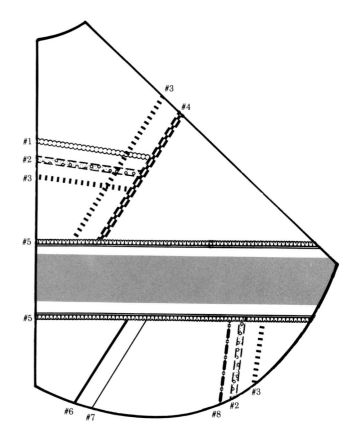

1 square = 1″

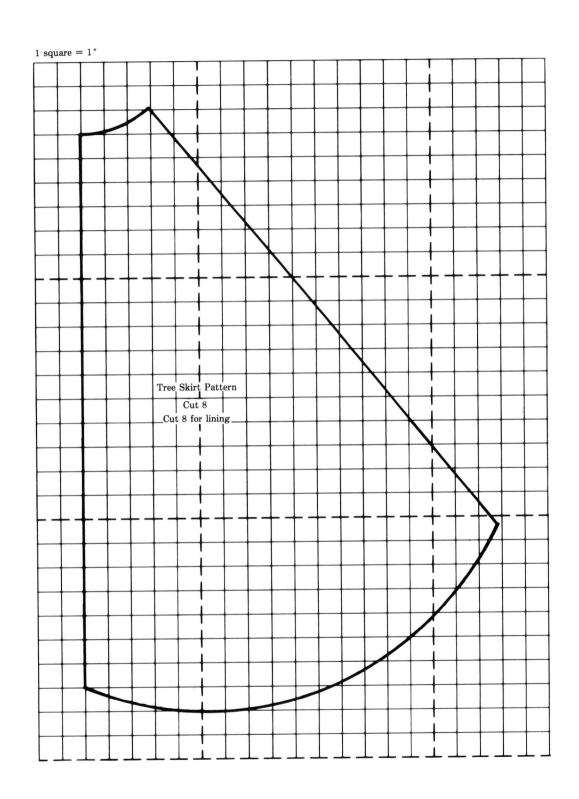

Tree Skirt Pattern
Cut 8
Cut 8 for lining

MATERIALS for stocking

Completed cross-stitch on white Belfast Linen 32; matching thread
⅝ **yard of linen-like white fabric**
⅝ **yard of white fabric for lining**
1½ **yards of silver picot trim**
1½ **yards of ¼″-wide assorted white flat trim**
6″ **of ⅛″-wide silver metallic ribbon**
200 **clear round beads**
125 **clear tube-shaped beads**
8 **copper donut-shaped beads**
4 **silver star beads**
Tracing paper for pattern
Dressmakers' pen

All seam allowances are ¼″.

1 Enlarge and trace the pattern for the stocking. From the linen-like fabric, cut two stocking pieces and one 2″ × 4″ piece for loop. From the white fabric, cut two stocking pieces for lining.

2 Place the 9½″ design strip on the top edge of the stocking front. Place the 18″ design strip diagonally from the left edge to the toe; see photo. Stitch in place, folding under ¼″ on all edges except top of stocking. Trim the ends of the strips to match the edges of the stocking front. Add silver picot trim to all long edges of design strips. Experiment with the placement of the trims, ribbon and beads working in diagonals; see photo. Then mark placement and stitch in place.

3 Stitch the right sides of the stocking front and back together. Clip curves and turn. Fold the loop piece in half, to measure 1″ × 4″, and stitch along the 4″ edge. Turn. Fold in half to make loop. Aligning raw edges, pin the loop to the top left edge of the stocking back.

4 Stitch the right sides of the lining pieces together. Slide the lining over the stocking with right sides together, matching side seams. Stitch together around the top edge, leaving a 3″ opening. Clip curves of lining and turn the stocking through the opening. Slipstitch the opening closed.

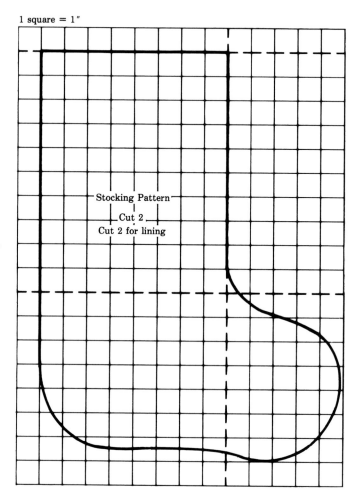

1 square = 1″

Stocking Pattern
Cut 2
Cut 2 for lining

186

GENERAL INSTRUCTIONS

CROSS-STITCH

Fabrics: Counted cross-stitch is usually worked on even-weave fabric. These fabrics are manufactured specifically for counted thread embroidery and are woven with the same number of vertical as horizontal threads per inch. Because the number of threads in the fabric is equal in each direction, each stitch will be the same size. It is the number of threads per inch in even-weave fabrics that determines the size of a finished design.

Preparing Fabric: Cut even-weave fabric at least 3″ larger on all sides than the design size or cut it the size specified in the sample paragraph. A 3″ margin is the minimum amount of space that allows for working the edges of the design comfortably. If the item is to be finished into a sachet bag, for example, the fabric should be cut as directed. To keep fabric from fraying, whip stitch or machine zigzag the raw edges.

Needles: Needles should slip easily through the holes in the fabric but not pierce the fabric. Use a blunt tapestry needle, size 24 or 26. Never leave the needle in the design area of your work. It can leave rust or a permanent impression on your fabric.

Floss: All numbers and color names are cross referenced between Anchor and DMC brands of six-strand embroidery floss. Cut 18″ lengths of floss. Run the floss over a damp sponge to straighten. Separate all six strands and use the number of strands called for in the code.

Centering Design: Find the center of the fabric by folding it in half horizontally and then vertically. Place a pin in the fold point to mark the center. Locate the center of the design on the graph by following vertical and horizontal arrows. Begin stitching at the center point of the graph and the fabric.

Securing the Floss: Start by inserting your needle up from the underside of the fabric at your starting point. Hold 1″ of thread behind the fabric and stitch over it, securing with the first few stitches. To finish thread, run under four or more stitches on the back of the design. Never knot floss unless working on clothing.

Another method for securing floss is the waste knot. Knot your floss and insert your needle from the right side of the fabric about 1″ from the design area. Work several stitches over the thread to secure. Cut off the knot later.

Stitching: For a smooth cross-stitch, use the "push and pull" method. Push the needle straight down and completely through fabric before pulling up. Do not pull the thread tight. The tension should be consistent throughout, making the stitches even. Make one stitch for every symbol on the chart. To stitch in rows, work from left to right and then back. Half-crosses are used to make a rounded shape. Make the longer stitch in the direction of the slanted line.

Carrying Floss: To carry floss, weave floss under the previously worked stitches on the back. Do not carry your thread across any fabric that is not or will not be stitched. Loose threads, especially dark ones, will show through the fabric.

Twisted Floss: If floss is twisted, drop the needle and allow the floss to unwind itself. Floss will cover best when lying flat. Use thread no longer than 18″ because it will tend to twist and knot.

Cleaning Completed Work: When all stitching is complete, soak the completed work in cold water with a mild soap for 5 to 10 minutes. Rinse and roll work into a towel to remove excess water; do not wring. Place work face down on a dry towel and, with iron on a warm setting, iron until work is dry.

STITCHES

Cross-stitch: Make one cross for each symbol on the chart. Bring needle and thread up at A, down at B, up at C, and down again at D.

For rows, stitch from left to right, then back. All stitches should lie in the same direction.

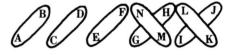

Half-cross: Make the longer stitch in the direction of the slanted line on the graph. The stitch actually fits three-fourths of the area. Bring needle and thread up at A, down at B, up at C, and down at D.

187

Backstitch: Complete all cross-stitching before working back stitches or other accent stitches. Working from left to right with one strand of floss (unless designated otherwise in code), bring needle and thread up at A, down at B, and up again at C. Going back down at A, continue in this manner.

French Knot: Bring the needle up at A, using one strand of embroidery floss. Wrap floss around needle two times. Insert needle beside A, pulling floss until it fits snugly around needle. Pull needle through to back.

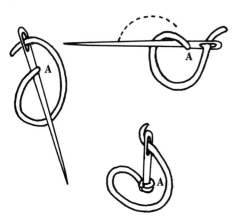

Beadwork: Attach beads to fabric with a half-cross, lower left to upper right. Secure beads by returning thread through beads, lower right to upper left. Complete row of half-crosses before returning to secure all beads.

Waste Canvas: Cut the waste canvas 1″ larger on all sides than the finished design size. Baste the waste canvas to the fabric or paper to be stitched. Complete the stitching. Each stitch is over one thread. When stitching is complete, use a spray bottle to dampen the stitched area with cold water. Pull the waste canvas threads out one at a time with tweezers. It is easier to pull all the threads running in one direction first; then pull out the opposite threads. Allow the stitching to dry; then place face down on a towel and iron.

SEWING HINTS

Slipstitch: Insert needle at A, slide it through the folded edge of the fabric for about ⅛″ to ¼″ and bring it out at B. Directly below B, take a small stitch through the second piece of fabric.

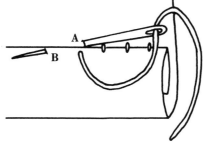

Clipping Seams: Clipping seam allowances is necessary on all curves, points, and most corners so that the finished seam will lie flat. Clip into the seam allowance at even intervals, ¼″ to ½″ apart, being careful not to cut through the stitching.

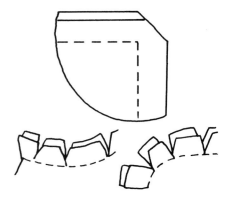

Bias Strips: Bias strips are used for ruffles, binding, or corded piping. To cut bias, fold the fabric at a 45-degree angle to the grain of the fabric and crease. Cut on the crease Cut additional strips the width indicated in instructions and parallel to the first cutting line. The ends of the bias strips should be on the grain of the fabric. Place the right sides of the ends together and stitch with a ¼″-seem. Continue to piece the strips until they are the length that is indicated in instructions.

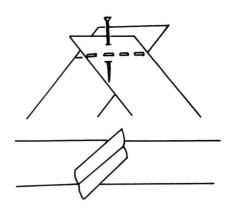

Corded Piping: Piece bias strips together to equal the length needed for cording. Place the cord in the center of the wrong side of the strip and fold the fabric over it. Using a zipper foot, stitch close to the cord through both layers of fabric. Trim the seam allowance ¼" from the stitching line.

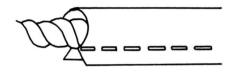

Gathering: Machine-stitch two parallel rows of long stitches ¼" and ½" from the edge of fabric (unless instructions say differently). Leave the ends of the thread 2" or 3" long. Pull the two bobbin threads and gather to fit the desired length. Long edges may need to be gathered from both ends. Disperse the fullness evenly and secure the threads in the seam by wrapping them around a pin in a figure eight.

VARNISHING

1 Trim the design piece so that it is 1" larger than the design on all sides. Cut the fusible web and the print fabric for the back the same size as the design piece. Fuse the design piece to the backing, according to the manufacturer's directions.

2 Varnish both sides of the design piece. Pin the edges to waxed paper and allow to dry for at least one hour.

3 Cut carefully, ⅛" outside of the stitching, following the general shape of the design.

4 Varnish again, covering the raw edges thoroughly. Allow to dry.

5 Spray both the front and the back surfaces with the glitter spray. Allow to dry.

CROCHET

Asterisk * and Number # – both used to mark the beginning and end of a set of instructions that are to be repeated.

Brackets [ ] – instructions are put inside brackets and these are to be repeated the number of times stated.

Cluster – two or more stitches, made leaving the last loop of each temporarily on the hook, until finally one loop is drawn through them all joining them together into one stitch at their top.

Decrease – lessening the number of stitches in a row.

Picot – a run of chain stitches fixed into a decorative loop to form a simple edging.

Abbreviations

beg	beginning
ch	chain
ch-	refers to chain previously made
dc	double crochet
hdc	half double crochet
rnd	round
sc	single crochet
sk	skip
sp	space
sl st	slipstitch
st	stitch

189

SUPPLIERS

All products are available retail from Shepherd's Bush, 220 24th Street, Ogden, UT 84401; (801) 399-4546; or for a merchant near you, write the following suppliers:

Zweigart Fabrics:
Aida 14 (Cream, Ash Rose)
Aida 18 (Cream)
Damask Aida 18 (Carnation Pink, Ivory)
Hardanger 22 (White, Cream)
Dublin Linen 25 (White, Cream, Blue, Sand, Pink)
Belfast Linen 32 (White, Cream, Raw, Driftwood)
Lugana 25 (Cream, Ash Rose, Pewter, Moss Green, Mushroom)
Bondeno (Cream)
Murano 30 (Pewter)
Waste Canvas 14
Quaker Cloth 28 (White)
Shonfels Damask 11 (Cream)
Davos 18 (Mushroom)

Zweigart/Joan Toggit Ltd., 35 Fairfield Place, West Caldwell, NJ 07006

Jobelan 28 (White, Ivory, Tan, Light Gray)
Wichelt Imports, Inc., Rural Route 1, Stoddard, WI 54658

Linaida 14, Soft Touch 14 (Mint Parfait)
Charles Craft, P.O. Box 1049, Laurinburg, NC 28352

Glenshee Linen (Green)
Anne Powell Heirloom Stitchery, P.O. Box 3060, Stuart, FL 33495

Perforated Paper (White, Cream)
Astor Place, 239 Main Avenue, Stirling, NJ 07980

Silk Gauze 40, Balger Thread
Kreinik Manufacturing, P.O. Box 1966, Parkersburg, WV 26101

Marlitt Thread
Joan Toggitt Ltd., 35 Fairfield Place, West Caldwell, NJ 07006

Flower Thread
Ginnie Thompson Guild, P.O. Box 465, Pawleys Island, SC 29585

Beads (MPR)
Gay Bowles Sales, Inc., P.O. Box 1060, Janesville, WI 53547

Candlescreen, Wood Box
Sudberry House, Box 895, Old Lyme, CT 06371

Perfume Tray, Lockets, Porcelain Jar
Anne Brinkley Designs, Inc., 21 Ransom Road, Newton Centre, MA 02159

Bell Pull Hardware
Feldman Enterprises, 4215 Alta Vista Lane, Dallas, TX 75229

Fireplace Screen
Freeman Manufacturing, Inc. P.O. Box 382, Thomasville, NC 27388

Small Stool
Plain 'n' Fancy, P.O. Box 357, Mathews, VA 23109

Silk Ribbon
Yarn Loft International Corp., 45 West 300 North, Provo, UT 84601

Ribbon
C. M. Offray & Son, Route 24, Box 601, Chester NJ 07930-0601

INDEX

All of us at Sedgewood® Press are dedicated to offering you, our customer, the best books we can create. We are particularly concerned that all of the instructions for making the projects are clear and accurate. We welcome your comments and would like to hear any suggestions you may have. Please address your correspondence to Customer Service Department, Sedgewood® Press, Meredith Corporation, 750 Third Avenue, New York, Ny 10017

The Idea Magazine for Better Homes and Families

For information on how you can have *Better Homes and Gardens* delivered to your door, write to: Mr. Robert Austin, P.O. Box 4536, Des Moines, IA 50336.